Starting out in Eventing

Hans-Peter Scheunemann

Starting out
in Eventing

An introduction to having fun cross country

CADMOS

Copyright of original edition © 2008 by Cadmos Verlag GmbH,

Im Dorfe 11, 22946 Brunsbek, Germany

Copyright of this edition © 2008 by Cadmos Books, Great Britain

Translation: Claire Lilley

Design and layout: Ravenstein + Partner

Typesetting: Nadine Hoenow

Cover photo: Jochen Becker

Photos without copyright notice: Jochen Becker

Drawings: Maria Mähler

Editorial: Anneke Bosse, Christopher Long

Printed by: agensketterl Druckerei, Mauerbach

British Library Cataloguing in Publication Data

A catalogue record of this book is available from the British Library.

Printed in Austria

ISBN 978-3-86127-957-0

www.cadmos.co.uk

Contents

Foreword

The predominant aim of all riders is to achieve harmony with their horses, particularly when riding out cross country, which is the horse's natural environment in the wild. All too often there is little help available for riders who either ride cross country as a sport or enjoy hacking out for pleasure, though this form of riding is a very popular form of equestrianism. Another aspect is when riding out in a group. The larger the group of riders, the more important it is for every rider to have a sound basic training. This author is very skilled at putting himself in the position of every rider and trainer in order to understand their needs, and to encourage the use of 'the great outdoors' as a training medium and without limiting schooling to the confines of an indoor school.

Technological development has changed the way in which we use horses. Riding enthusiasts often lose awareness about, or misunderstand the nature of, the horse and its needs. Their quest for 'improvement' often involves training methods that are far removed from the ideal, to the detriment of the horse's well-being, both mentally and physically. This also applies to many experienced competition riders who have the opportunity to train cross country, but who do not have access to proper training that respects the horse's needs. Having the wrong trainer can have a detrimental effect on the rider's inspiration, and he will lose out on the benefits that correct and logical cross-country training can offer.

There are all too few 'horsemen' nowadays with the experience of Hans-Peter Scheunemann who enjoys educating all riders, whatever their age or experience. His vast experience is invaluable in offering solutions to training problems and to develop the rider's ability.

The many popular 'Scheunemann clinics' are legendary; they have helped numerous riders to improve their cross-country skills. Riders acquire motivation, improved ability, and greater knowledge and harmony with their horses, which all contribute to their safe enjoyment of the sport.

This book is long overdue. Every reader will be inspired to consider the nature of the horse, and take more of an interest in training. This philosophy lies in the heart and hands of every good trainer. This book is much more than its title,

Starting out in Eventing; it is a comprehensive training manual for every riding instructor, following the principles of classical training, from basic level upwards, for every horse and rider.

Hans-Peter Scheunemann has the benefit of practical experience as a trainer and judge and has developed a profound knowledge and understanding about the nature of the horse through his work. I have learnt a lot more myself when previewing this book. I am pleased to say that the information given is in accordance with my own experience.

This book deserves to become a standard reference title for cross-country riding, and much to the well-being of the horse and enjoyment for the rider.

Martin Plewa, German National Eventing Coach, 1984–2000, February 2008

Introduction

Many so-called competition riders, and also hobby-riders, lock themselves away in a dusty, and often busy, indoor school, even in the summer months. Others may venture outside into a dusty, narrow and unfenced outdoor school. Both groups are a danger to themselves and their horses should they attempt to ride across country.

Systematic cross-country riding is seldom taught in riding schools and riding clubs. There is no desire, need or effort to do so. Cross-country riding is grossly under-estimated. There are trainers who are willing to pass on their experience to others. Their job is to convince anxious parents and horse owners that riding cross country does not have to be dangerous. Many riders do not learn how easy it is to ride in balance and to develop a 'feel' for their horses. They miss out on the wonderful experience of riding forwards in a controlled manner in the horse's natural environment.

"The riding instructor's arena is the open countryside. In this situation, the pupil must put into practice everything he has learnt."

(Waldemar Seunig)

The aim of cross-country training is to be able to ride across country, alone or in a group, in a controlled manner.

This book fills a void in the training of every horse and rider. It is educational for the parents of children who ride, as it explains the value of riding cross country. It is of interest to every equestrian sportsman, regardless of age group, who spends every weekend at a showground, either competing in dressage or show jumping. It is all too easy to forget what a great experience it can be to ride out in the sunshine as part of the preparation for competition. It is valuable for all riders who spend their free time with their horses, adding an alternative to just going to endless competitions.

Everyone should have the chance to enjoy being on horseback in the countryside. Being able to ride well cross country is as much of an achievement as winning a rosette.

This book is not for beginners. It is presumed that the reader will already have received basic training. Every rider should be familiar with and know how to ride using the six scales of training: rhythm, suppleness, contact, impulsion, straightness and collection. Without the scales of training, a rider can spend years and years without actually achieving anything. The scales of training evolved in order to develop the ride-ability of the horse, and a high level of confidence, which is essential for successful cross-country riding. The basic rules of classical training in this book are nothing new, in fact, they are 'everything that has been spoken or written for over a thousand years'.

(Helmut Beck-Broichsitter)

Definition of eventing

Eventing in competition is made up of three parts: dressage, cross country and show jumping. This book concentrates on the cross country section, which is most often associated with eventing. The other two sections play an important part in the basic training for successful cross-country riding.

Both people and animals have a fear of the unknown. An unfounded dread of riding cross country comes from our alienation with nature, but it only takes the touch of a button to change fear into fun.

This alienation of people from nature is often seen from the way they care and manage their horses. Most trainers and riders shun the countryside as a training medium, seeing danger around every corner, but the way forwards is to include cross-country riding in every horse's training programme.

Statistics show that more accidents happen around the stable yard or in the field than when riding cross country. For this reason, the horse's characteristics and attitude are explained here, as well as behaviour and training. Training in cross-country riding requires comprehensive equestrian knowledge, including saddlery, and awareness of safety issues relevant to the horse and the rider. Cross-country riding is natural for horse and rider. This is well-founded; the oldest breed of horse, the Arab, is known as the 'Drinker of the Wind'.

Cross-country riding is natural for horse and rider.
Well-thought-out facilities make it possible to train using a huge variety of options.

What is cross-country riding?

Educated cross-country riding means that horse and rider can travel effortlessly, safely and comfortably across the natural surroundings of the horse. This is the meaning of harmony between horse and rider. This forms the foundation of basic training for every horse and every rider who is responsible for his charge; a variety of work is healthy, exercising all parts of the horse equally. Basic training is essential preparation for the horse and (young) rider before specialising in any particular discipline.

The development of eventing as a sport

The horse has been used by man as means of transport for about 5,000 years. It was a pack animal before being ridden at a later stage. There were no proper roads or bridleways in those days. Every ride was a hack. Over time, the demands placed on the horse were changed, for instance, by the onset of war. A riding system was developed due to the demands of the military. Safely mounted soldiers were as important as gunpowder for the weapons. The gun could only fire once; then the soldier had to ride for his life in order to reload. That is why nimble horses were needed. The rideability of the horse could make the difference between life and death. Today, this is known as dressage. Friedrich II, King of Prussia, and Reitgeneral Seydlitz made a rule that stood for over 200 years:

"The horse must be made free in the shoulder so that a Hussar and his horse can turn on the spot as small as a coin wherever he wants when riding across country."

On the one hand, this meant that the whole regiment should be capable of performing canter pirouettes. On the other hand, by introducing the dressage phase in addition to cross country in military training, the riding sport known as eventing was born, which was also called 'military', in reference to the beginnings of this sport. The Campagneschule, a riding establishment (1750–1800) established by Seydlitz, represented the philosophy of developing speed, mobility and safety across country.

The Campagneschule, which taught cross-country riding and show jumping, also developed as a training centre for school riding, or dressage.

The aim was always to produce a horse that was safe and careful across country. This could not come about only using the previous system of training, so in the 1900s they learnt from the Italian Federico Caprilli:

"The main goal of the rider is to be fast and safe when riding across country. It is essential for the rider to learn that going too fast causes fatigue, which works against him, and that periods of calmness and gentleness prolong power and strength."

(Federico Caprilli)

The natural training methods of Caprilli and the forward or jumping seat are important in their own right in any training system. However, together with the development of gymnastic dressage training, this system was taken up by the Cavalry School in Hanover, which has a history of world-wide sporting success. The basic rules of this system were laid down in a manuscript in 1912 (HDV12) and are the forerunner of today's German Rules for Riding and Driving. The Second World War caused a break in training development in 1939. After 1945, this training method was resumed by equestrian personnel such as Max Habel, a German national eventing trainer from 1968 to 1980. From him came the expression 'educated cross-country riding'.

Federico Caprilli developed the 'forward seat' at the beginning of the 20th century.

Prior to that, one would lean back over a fence, not taking best care for the horse (Photos: Cadmos)

Max Habel, German National Eventing trainer from 1968 to 1980 promotes educated cross-country riding. (Photo: private)

Cross-country riding today

Today, cross-country riding is predominantly a pleasure activity and gives riders an opportunity to put their training into practice.

After the end of the Second World War, and through advances in technology and society, equestrianism developed as a sport, giving people the opportunity to spend leisure time with horses, or for sports training. Cross-country riding gave riders the opportunity to put their training into practice:

- Familiarising the horse with different situations and ground surfaces
- Schooling uphill and downhill
- Ignoring distractions
- Building trust by riding through or jumping over water
- Developing balance between horse and rider
- Improving ride-ability and riding skill
- Developing expertise and speed of reactions
- Gymnastic and fitness work for the horse
- Canter work and developing a feel for tempo
- Changing tempo and direction
- Familiarity with cross-country obstacles
- Improving condition

Successful cross-country training opens many opportunities for the hobby or competition rider:

- Hacking out in walk (turning a trudge in the countryside into gymnastic work)
- Hacking out on long rides long-distance riding, building power and condition)
- Riding out with the hunt
- Taking part in competitions

Taking part in a long ride or distance riding or riding out with an organised hunt can help with further specialised training. Hacking out for pleasure and including a few gymnastic exercises is enjoyable for every horse and uplifting for the rider's spirit.

The type of cross-country riding depends on the individual and each rider's personal goal, which should be to be ride with ease, safely and in comfort, at whatever level they rides.

Today, cross-country riding is predominantly a pleasure activity and gives riders an opportunity to put their training into practice. (Photo: Gero Kärst)

Rules for cross-country riding

Riding in the countryside, hacking out, is another use for farmland, streets and bridleways, but it is dependent on traffic, the landowner, hikers and many other factors. For safety reasons, you should be aware of any restrictions and rules that apply where you wish to ride. Information on bridleways and where to ride can be obtained through the British Horse Society, Stoneleigh Deer Park, Kenilworth, Warwickshire, CV8 2XZ

Training outdoors in natural surroundings

The natural lie of the land can be of help to the riding instructor. It gives the opportunity to develop the horse's health and well-being and to school the horse for ride-ability following the scales of training, as well as developing the rider's seat and aids. Balance and suppleness of horse and rider are the basis for developing rhythm and contact. There is no more pleasurable way of learning. If training is fun, it is easy.

Horses that are only schooled on well-maintained surfaces will trip up over the smallest molehill.

For this reason, it is just as important for the horse to learn where to put its feet in the countryside as well as in the arena. Looking at this in another way, the horse that is surefooted in the countryside has no problem in an arena. It can step confidently as it has developed the intelligence to remain in balance regardless of the surface.

The horse can learn to use its back and to carry a rider without the use of an outdoor school or and indoor arena. Under a skilled rider, straightness and suppleness develop simply due to the demands placed on the horse when riding cross country, and as a result, it learns to work into a secure contact. Impulsion and collection come from riding up- and downhill. Specialised dressage work does not need to have a set training plan in the beginning; it can develop from cross-country riding.

Many exercises and movements that may cause horse and rider difficulty in the arena are easily tackled in the countryside. Riding over uneven ground is not only useful for the event rider. The ridden demands placed on the horse cross country are more so than in a dressage arena. Educated cross-country riding helps the horse and rider to achieve their goals without much effort. Cross-

Riding straight downhill has a dramatic collecting effect, through which the young horse learns on its own to carry weight behind.

Training for competition

The demands of eventing as a sport require a comprehensive training regime. It is the pinnacle of equestrianism, even in its present form, which no longer requires the steeplechase phase and has fewer long stretches at the gallop.

In the French language, one would call this 'concours complet' or a complete competition. Any omissions in the horse's training for the three disciplines of dressage, cross country and show jumping will come to light. Success in eventing is not about winning or being placed, but about completing the competition. This success comes about from the trust between horse and rider, and their unity throughout the training and the event itself. This requires a great deal of discipline. Keeping the three elements separate during training requires a lot of discipline, but specialising too early in any one can be detrimental to the horse's overall progress.

This book is not about eventing as a competition. The details about training and specific schooling issues that are included are about educated cross-country riding. Eventing as a sport requires the fundamental basics of training that can be developed in the natural surroundings of the horse, i.e., outside in all weathers. The pleasure and natural impulsion that come with regularly riding outside are of great benefit when riding in the dressage arena or show-jumping course.

Through regular cross-country work, the pupil learns how to cope with the horse's reactions in various situations and to different experiences. He achieves a greater understanding of the horse's character and behaviour through daily handling, as well as under saddle. Comprehensive basic training also develops the horse's character and overall competence, as well as communication between

Riding cross country as part of all-round basic training can also be included in competition for even the youngest rider. (Photo: Johann Wachruschew)

country work is useful for every discipline of equestrian sport. It saves many horses from being ridden in draw reins or other such gadgets. Specialising in a particular discipline too early can cause a breakdown of horse and rider and bring their progress to a standstill. The demands of cross-country riding easily improve the pupil's seat and aids.

"Everyone who is stuck within the four walls of a riding school becomes singleminded, stuffy and even dopey, and causes their horse to lose the will to live."

(Felix Bürkner)

rider and horse. One of the most important jobs of the riding instructor is to get the best from his pupils. This takes a combination of knowledge, awareness, feel and experience. As the pupil progresses, he should gradually need less help and guidance from his teacher.

The sporting demands of riding

Cross-country riding does not only ask questions of the horse, but is also physically demanding for the rider. A rider who is weak and tired is a much heavier burden for the horse to carry. This rider is unable to help the horse as his aids are ineffective, and he becomes a burden to the horse instead of working as a partnership. This puts both horse and rider in danger and there is a greater risk of injury.

All-round physical training for the rider is the same as in any other sport requiring physical fitness attributes such as stamina, strength, alertness, ease of movement, athleticism, condition and co-ordination. All these are required to improve the welfare of the horse. Riding as a sport requires the rider to be warmed up as well as the horse.

More about this is on page 65.

Cantering uphill is excellent gymnastic work and develops power from behind, useful not only for cross country, but also in the dressage arena.

Ground rules for the rider

The basic rules of riding are dependent on the relationship between horse and rider. The horse is fundamentally a prairie dweller, prey and a flight animal. Man, primarily a cave dweller and hunter, is merely a guest on the horse's back. The two are so different that it seems impossible for them to work together. Within the realm of this book, it is impossible to do justice to such a subject, but certain aspects are covered as they are so relevant for developing trust and safety when riding across country.

Ground rules for training the horse

The movement of the horse can be made more powerful and beautiful only through so-called 'classical training' and skilled riding. Riding instructors have been around for 1000 years and have developed further from the teachings of Xenophon over 450 years ago. His basic rules are given below.

Three elements of
the system of teaching horsemanship:
- *Gymnastic exercises for the horse following the scales of training.*
- *Gradual progression throughout the training of horse and rider without the constraints of time pressure.*
- *Improving the riding ability of the rider.*

A skilled rider should be competent and be able to combine knowledge and ability. He should have developed a good basic seat and have the experience to give effective aids. He should be able to overcome with ease the physical and mental issues that the body finds unnatural when riding.

He should understand the relationship between the skill of the rider and the ride-ability of the horse, and how the rider's weight influences the balance of the horse when ridden.

The riding instructor should clearly explain the rules of riding without deviating from the right way to reach the final goal. The most important aim is to develop harmony between horse and rider while helping them to progress.

A skilled rider should be competent and be able to combine knowledge and ability. He should have developed a good basic seat and have the experience to give effective aids. He should be able to overcome with ease the physical and mental issues that the body finds unnatural when riding. He should understand the relationship between the skill of the rider and the ride-ability of the horse, and how the rider's weight influences the balance of the horse when ridden.

The riding instructor should clearly explain the rules of riding without deviating from the right way to reach the final goal. The most important aim is to develop harmony between horse and rider while helping them to progress.

The riding instructor has to deal with every horse, every rider and every riding situation that could arise. This should be developed by studying the nature of horses and making the relationship between man and horse easier. The physical development of the horse is important whatever field of equestrianism the horse is destined for. Work from the ground is an important part of training and brings many possibilities to the improvement of the horse. This has little to do with training the horse under saddle. It can be beneficial to overcome issues such as nervousness, kicking or fear, and gives man an opportunity to understand the psychology of the horse. This is different from gymnastic physical work, though.

The classical training of horse and rider plays a great part in riding safely across country and preventing the horse from getting into difficulty or becoming injured.

Inexperienced riders should be taught cross country riding in the classical way by an experienced trainer.

Knowledge, talent and feel

Riders often ask why their horses do not make progress as quickly as they would like. The answer lies in the nature of people, demonstrated in the following quote:

"A characteristic of people is to always blame something else, even God. This happens when an animal does not do what the person wants. It is common to say 'It is never the rider's fault,' blaming the horse and not the rider, in this situation."

(Eberhard Trumler)

A second answer to the question lies in the personality of the horse. It may simply be because the horse does not want to co-operate. A horse will not go against the rider, providing that the rider is first in rank. The horse's behaviour has nothing to do with being interested in what people want; the horse does not always do what it is expected to. The horse behaves instinctively in a situation: for instance loading into a trailer, where water is located or where to find hay. There are three aspects to dealing with resistance in the horse: being over-faced; fear; or misunderstanding. Over-facing the horse is the fault of the incompetent rider. Fear comes from the horse's natural flight reflex to defend itself against predators. The rider requires feel and knowledge in order to overcome this without affecting its natural caution and awareness. Misunderstanding is one of the greatest causes of lack of harmony between horse and rider, affecting their progress. Horses communicate with each other primarily with body language. The rider communicates with the horse by body language by using his seat and aids. Every horse can learn to understand this language.

"The art of riding is about reaching an understanding with the horse."

(Felix Bürkner)

Correction rather than punishment

Not everything always goes well and in harmony when training animals. Training riding horses is an art. Making mistakes along the way is part of the learning process, but sometimes these errors of judgement can cause the horse discomfort, stress or even physical pain. The biological meaning of pain is that it acts as a red warning light or alarm. Dr Peter Cronau describes it as a 'the bark of a watchdog'. Fear is closely related to pain. Both of these will cause the horse to become badly behaved, especially if it is in a situation where it cannot run away (flight instinct) or attack. A horse will not forget fear or pain in its lifetime.

Pain has a detrimental effect on the training of the horse and should be avoided at all costs. Morally, training has to be based on wisdom and knowledge, and not by causing the horse any harm. Training a riding horse in the right way does not always go smoothly. There will be misunderstandings and mistakes, but the important thing is to learn from these situations and to obtain a greater understanding of the psychology of the horse.

"You will make progress with the horse once you both speak the same language."

(Gustav Steinbrecht)

The young horse must be given time to get used to new experiences cross country.
Punishing a horse for stopping at a ditch is fruitless – it will only cause mistrust of the rider.

The ability of the rider to correct the horse and the ability of the horse to accept correction are the fundamental goals of successful training. Training the horse successfully requires systematic work, which depends on the rider's feel and ability to assess the horse's requirements throughout.

For the horse to be managed successfully, it needs care and respect, praise and reward, as well as correction by reprimand or punishment. All these criteria are related to the horse's natural instincts. The main principle of successful horse management is to establish the pecking order with the trainer being top 'rank' above the horse. Trying to correct a horse without punishing it is a weakness in the eyes of the horse. Reprimand is an important part of training, providing it is based on sound knowledge and experience. Correctly done, this has a positive effect; Incorrectly done, reprimanding too severely or too weakly will be a negative experience for the horse and trust will be lost. For this reason, it is very important to reprimand the horse immediately, within a matter of seconds. The horse will not understand if it is left too late, the whole thing becomes a negative experience, and the horse's trust will be lost. It is most important to work with the horse and not against it, and to maintain harmony and lightness at all times.

How to correct the horse

1. Positive and negative aspects:

Ride forwards: each correction should not affect the forward movement, which includes collected work to improve lightness. Half-halts: the classical way to improve the horse's way of going, half-halts can be used as a correction for negative behaviour such as going against the rider.

2. Basically positive aspects:

Adding variety: by varying the contents and location of the training programme. Knowing when to stop: taking a step backwards in the training, taking a break, ceasing an exercise are only seldom used. When the horse has understood what is required, the training should end for the day, and it should be allowed to stretch on a long rein. Always end on a good note, even if the exercise has not been totally successful. There has to be flexibility to allow for problems, and in this situation it is important not to stick too rigidly to the programme. The goal is to end on a good note and to build the horse's trust.

3. Basically negative aspects:

Riding too strongly forwards and strong half-halts are both uncomfortable for the horse and unnecessary. Aggressive aids, either with the whip, spurs or the voice, are not helpful to the horse's progress.

In order for the horse to progress, the rider, as long-term trainer of his horse, must be able to recognise early signs of success or failure, and be able to adapt the training accordingly.

'I have time." I would like all riders to take heed of this saying and deal with any difficulties immediately in order to maintain harmony with the horse.'

(Alois Podhajski)

It would be foolish for an inexperienced rider to try to train a horse without the help of a knowledgeable trainer. A rider without a sound basic knowledge may not notice shortfalls in the horse's training and fail to recognise faulty equipment, and may fail to ensure that the horse is healthy and fit. The horse has an instinctive fear of the unknown. Progress can only be made if the rider acts immediately in any adverse situation and if the horse understands what is expected of it. The horse will also be afraid if the rider is angry or impatient. If the horse does not understand what the rider asks through poor training, its sense of self-preservation takes over and it becomes afraid, and goes against the rider. This can be dangerous, so care must be taken to avoid such a situation.

"One should never be thoughtless and act in anger. It is the rider's duty to treat the horse with kindness every time it has done what has been asked. This is the best way for the horse to learn." (Xenophon)

It is all too easy for things to go wrong when preparing the horse for competition, or in the warm-up arena. In understanding the psychology of the horse, it is important to make any correction without force, ambition or vanity.

Bettina Eistel, who has won silver medals at the World Championships and in the Paralympics, shows here that having a disability does not detract from being an event rider. (Photo: Marianne Lins)

One should keep one's self-control in all circumstances. Broadly speaking, a horse can achieve a great deal without being ridden with force or pressure, a good example of which can be seen with horses ridden in sport by disabled riders. Riders without arms or legs can take their horses to the highest levels of competition. Simple cross-country exercises are all it takes for such riders to reach an affinity with their horses. This should also apply to able-bodied riders. Great achievements can be made without the horse being made to suffer in the process.

Pecking order, submission and harmony

Obedience and submission are the horse's acknowledgement of the rider's wishes. These are established through communication with the horse through the body language of the rider's set and aids. For the horse to obey the rider, the rider must be higher in the pecking order than the horse. Man should recognise the first signs of adverse behaviour by the horse and react accordingly. The fact is that a horse in pain will not howl like a dog, so it is difficult to know how it is feeling. The amateur trainer will not notice the subtle signs of discomfort, and, because the horse shows no obvious signs of pain, assume that all is well and carry on regardless.

This goes hand in hand with the current discussions about 'over-bending' and 'learned helplessness' or 'learned dullness'. If a horse could wag its tail like a dog or purr like a cat, it would be far easier to tell how the horse is feeling.

"Horses have no way of showing pain. Submission to a hard hand is the horse's way of shouting for help as loudly as it can."
(Dr Gerd Heuschmann)

It is often hard to distinguish between pain and disobedience. Only when you know the horse well enough to understand the subtle signals given by the ears can you tell whether the horse is confused by the rider's aids, aggressive or in pain.

The rider must be 'herd leader' for the horse in order to gain its trust.
This is essential when faced with challenging situations such as here, jumping a ditch and brush fence.

The horse's world is governed by the herd. The rider must be a part of that herd, and be higher in the pecking order than the horse. In order to gain the horse's trust, you need to think like a horse. Once the horse trusts you, it makes life far easier, especially when visits from the vet or farrier are necessary. You need to know the horse well in order to feed and handle it in the right way.

Teaching the horse to accept you as 'herd leader' is dependent on how it is done. The horse must have absolute trust in your authority so that it 'follows the herd' without wanting to take evasive action. Having authority depends very much on the way you behave towards the horse. There must be understanding and trust. You should not be unclear, unsure, vague, inconsistent or in a hurry.

A loss of authority alters the pecking order, and it can be caused by inconsistent handing: for example, being rough one minute and mollycoddling the next. If the pecking order is clear, the horse is compliant and understands what is required. This is essential for making progress with the training, which surely must be the aim of the trainer, who must have the knowledge and experience to improve the horse's ability in a logical way. If the horse does not understand its place in the pecking order, it can become afraid or nervous, rear up, run away or take other such evasive actions. The horse is being neither disobedient nor aggressive; it simply does not respect your authority.

Obedience goes hand in hand with ride-ability, and is essential to the horse's education. An obedient horse trusts its trainer at all times, especially when put under pressure. If this is not so, then the horse loses confidence very quickly, which can be shown by spookiness, running away or napping. Submission and obedience can be restored once the pecking order is re-established.

The influence of the rider's seat

Just as important as the pecking order is the communication between horse and rider through the rider's seat and aids. This relationship is the basis of trust between horse and rider. The seat of the rider can be compared to the instrument of a musician, or the tools of a craftsman.

Principles of the rider's seat

The basic rules of a good seat have not changed since the teachings of Steinbrecht and Caprilli. A conventional, classical seat and a correct understanding of the aids play a significant part in developing the horse's suppleness and looseness. A good seat is essential for training the horse. For example, a crooked horse can make the rider crooked. If the rider is not experienced enough to notice this, then neither horse nor rider will ever be straight.

"The seat is dependent on a rider who has good posture and even muscle development on both sides. This is essential for the rider to be able to go with the horse in movement. If this is not so, small abnormalities must be corrected. A defective seat should never be neglected."
(Rule of riding for the Cavalry in 1912)

There is no such thing as the 'right' seat. The rider must instinctively do what is best for the horse and maintain harmony in any situation that arises. An incorrect or faulty seat is where the rider is not in balance with the horse, and exercises must be used to improve this. Maintaining balance over the horse's centre of gravity is a 'good' seat. In order to do this, sometimes the rider will be behind the vertical in order to keep weight into the stirrups and to stay with the horse. Many riders cannot feel if their seat is faulty, and can be convinced that they sit well even when they do not.

Faults are stored in the memory. It is not the muscles that must unlearn them, but the central nervous system. In order to develop a good seat, both horse and rider must be properly equipped (see page 57). Reins and stirrups must be the correct length.

There is an important relationship between posture and mental attitude. Looking closely at horse and rider can tell you in a moment how they relate to one another, both physically and mentally. A rider in harmony with the horse appears to be still in the saddle. This is essential for the rider. If the rider loses his posture, he loses balance and harmony with the horse.

A correct seat is where horse and rider are in balance, with the same centre of gravity.

On a well-trained horse, a classical, correct and supple seat is used for driving, collecting or bending. The seat accommodates the movement of the horse's back, absorbing energy and relaxation, with the legs lying quietly against the horse's sides, as though allowing the horse to breathe. The rider must be supple through his back sufficiently to move with the horse in walk, trot and canter, so that the horse goes confidently and willingly forwards.

A rider requires muscle tone and balance in order to move with the horse properly. To go with every movement of the horse requires contraction and relaxation of the muscles and the use of every joint in the body. Both physical and mental control need to be fine-tuned for the rider to react quickly and instinctively when necessary.

Muscle tone is essential to support the skeleton so that the body can function, both when standing still and when moving. Without muscle tone, the body will droop like a wilting plant. A rider without muscle tone will collapse in the saddle and feel like a dead weight to the horse.

Too much tension has an adverse effect on the gait of the horse. A tense rider will restrict the horse's movement and affect the suppleness of the horse's back.

The forward seat

The light seat is important for every cross-country rider and has many uses, such as when riding over ground poles, jumping training, for riding young horses and for warming up and cooling down. Before this was introduced, there was little understanding about how the seat affects the horse when jumping. In the first half of the 20th century, Caprilli discovered the forward seat, also known as the jumping or racing seat. Erich Christian Count Holck was the first rider to introduce this new seat to Germany, which made a great difference to riding in general.

"I studied the seat of the Count Holck:
his seat was higher than his face:
where he sat, no one could know."
(Unknown source, passed on
by Burkhard Beck-Broichsitter)

In the light seat, the horse can carry the weight of the rider plus the equipment without its movement being hindered in any way. The rider can accommodate any movement of the horse, allowing it to move freely through its back. The light seat gives the rider great security in the saddle, particularly when riding cross country. Correct use of the weight aids is very important in this seat.

To ride in a light seat correctly, the stirrups must be short enough. The best way to develop a secure seat is to ride regularly with short stirrups during training. In the light seat it is important to have the reins the correct length in order to maintain a steady contact with still hands. The hands should be placed on the crest of the neck in line with the rider's eyes, at about where the neck strap of a running martingale would be. With the hands in this position, it is easy to follow the move-

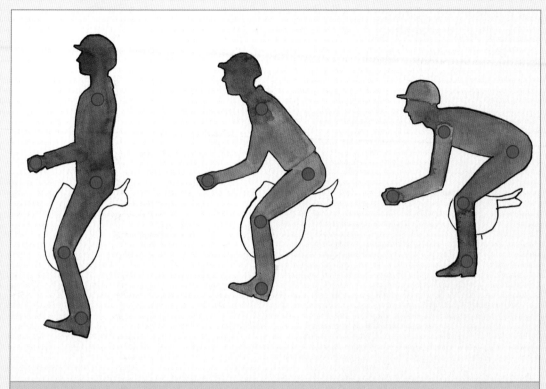

The rider's centre of gravity should be directly in line with the stirrups in the dressage seat (left),
in the light seat (middle) and the racing seat (right). The difference between them is the angle of the upper body.
A secure lower leg position ensures that the rider remains in balance.
The stirrups and reins must be the correct length.

ment of the horse's neck and to use both reins effectively. The hand position and rein aids should be independent of the rider's seat. If the reins are too long, the rider can have a tendency to sit too far back in a 'chair seat' in order to keep a contact with the horse's mouth. If the reins are too short, the rider can be drawn too far forwards into a 'fork seat' and get in front of the horse's movement, putting himself in danger of losing balance or even falling off.

The rider's weight should be divided between the saddle and the stirrups. This can easily be seen in the dressage seat. In a correct lower leg position with a lowered heel and the calves against the horse's sides, the ankle and knee joints act as shock absorbers, enabling the rider to sit quietly in the saddle. Flexibility in the ankle is lost if the heels are either drawn up or forced downwards. A balanced, light seat is only achievable with a correct lower leg position, which allows the rider to increase the weight in the stirrups.

When cantering in a light seat, the shorter the stirrups are, the easier it is for the rider to keep in balance with the horse. Stirrups that are too long may cause the lower legs to swing back and forward, result in an unsteady upper body position, and making it difficult for the rider to give effective leg aids.

A common problem is that the rider does not understand how to fold the upper body forwards from the hips in a correct way. Most just lean forwards, putting their weight over the horse's forehand, restricting the freedom of the horse's shoulders. Gripping with the knees can cause the lower legs to swing backwards.

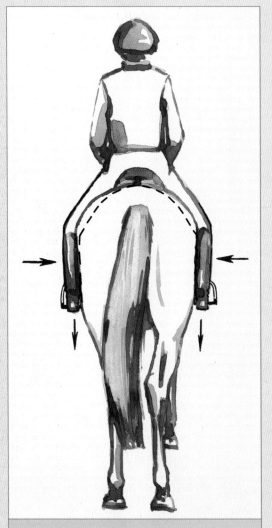

Leaning forwards with the upper body and gripping with the knees, allowing the lower legs to swing back, creates a 'false' light seat (above).

In the correct light seat (below), the rider's weight is kept over the stirrups by keeping the seat towards the back of the saddle and the lower leg under the body, maintaining the centre of gravity.

In this example of a good driving seat, the rider's legs exert a downwards pressure on the stirrups at the same time as pressing against the horse's sides, i.e., the leg aid is 'down and on'.

The faster the canter, the more the upper body must fold,
and the more the hips should be taken towards the rear of the saddle.

In this instance the rider will lean forwards, getting in front of the horse's movement and will no longer keep his weight into the stirrups, rendering the weight aids ineffective. Suppleness in the rider's upper body will be lost and the horse will no longer be in front of the rider's aids.

As in the dressage seat, a horse and rider in balance will have a combined centre of gravity. Keeping the weight off the horse's back correctly in the light seat means that the rider must maintain a straight vertical line between his shoulder, knee and ball of the foot. This only works if the breast bone is brought down towards the withers and the hips are taken towards the rear of the saddle, rather like the posture of a downhill skier, whose posterior is often over the back of the skis as he crouches down.

The height of the rider's centre of gravity above the horse depends on how low he is over the horse. The most extreme example is the jockey travelling at great speed, who lies very low over the horse's back.

Basic requirements for a light seat:

- *Vertical lower legs and a secure but flexible knee*

- *Hips taken towards the rear*

- *Seat on the saddle*

- *Low hands placed either side of the horse's crest (for bridging the reins, see photo on the right)*

- *Lowered shoulders, with the head lifted and looking forwards*

Establishing a light seat is just the beginning. The rider must then learn how to adapt his seat for different situations. The experienced rider knows how much to lean forwards at any one time, and how to remain safe and secure in the saddle so he can give effective weight aids and keep himself and his horse balanced. The horse must learn to work with the rider in a light seat. For the rider, this means practice – and lots of it. The seat should be established in trot first of all.

'Bridging the reins' means that the spare end of each rein passes through the opposite hand. This creates a bridge or short amount of each rein that can be held with a light pressure over the horse's neck by the withers. This gives the rider a handle to use should he lose his balance if the horse stumbles and prevents the hands jerking out of position. (Photo: Christiane Slawik)

The 'cavalry pose'.
Standing up with the hands behind the head is a very good way of learning how to balance with the weight in the stirrups.

Learning to balance with the hands forwards on the horse's neck is a good exercise for riders who bring their hands back behind the edge of the saddle. The lower legs must remain in contact with the horse's sides, under the centre of gravity. The upper body, shoulders and hands can quietly follow the horse's movement, which in turn helps the horse to relax its back. It is important that the rider keeps his weight into the stirrups.

The light seat can be practised effectively in trot, especially over ground poles or cavaletti.
It can also be useful to approach obstacles from trot in a light seat. Alternating between rising trot and
a light seat is another good exercise that can help horse and rider prepare for the unexpected,
improving confidence and balance, which are crucial for riding cross country.

The aids and the contact

The seat is correct when the rider is able to improve the horse's way of going. This requires good co-ordination on the rider's part between the application of the aids and their assessment or feel of the horse. The aids can be divided into supporting, forwards driving, sideways driving, bending and collecting. The aids are the same, whichever seat the rider adopts. The weight aids are often underused, and rein contact overused. A poor or misused contact with the horse's mouth, with the reins either too loose or too tight, can put the horse in danger. Cross country, all the aids must be effective in the light seat. The rider must learn to apply the aids in every type of seat. The effectiveness of the aids depends upon the rider's body control.

The importance and meaning of the aids:

- *Weight aids:*
  about 80% – riding with the seat
- *Leg aids:*
  about 15% – supporting with the legs
- *Rein aids:*
  about 5% – maintaining a steady contact

The whip and spurs should be used as corrective aids if the horse does not respond, but it is important that they are used correctly. They can be used to increase energy, to make sure the horse goes in the right direction, to maintain rhythm and to keep the horse working through to the contact. The whip, spurs and voice aids can be used to motivate the horse, but it is just as important to use the voice to praise the horse, for example, by saying 'Good boy', as it is to back up its reaction to the aids, such as saying 'Canter' as the aids are given.

Using the voice helps to build the horse's confidence in the rider, and can help the rider to remain calm. The horse may not understand every word the rider says, but it will certainly pick up the tone of voice, and know if he is cross, or in a good mood. Singing might help!

Clicking with the tongue and hissing to encourage the horse forwards work well, simply because the horse naturally takes notice of what is behind it. The horse picks up danger by hearing it rather than seeing it.

Contact means to give the horse confidence and security in any given situation.

39

Raising the upper body in the light seat acts as a half-halt and prepares the horse for the next situation.

Hissing sounds like a snake, so the horse will naturally want to run away from danger, hence it will go forwards to that particular aid. Going through a water splash or water jump can have a similar effect: the horse will want to get away from the noise.

The key to good riding is to maintain a correct contact, a subject that is so often misunderstood. Contact is as much to do with the rider's seat as it is the reins. It takes a good feel from a rider to keep a steady contact, and it is this steady contact that gives the horse a framework and stability.

There are occasions when the contact needs to be given away and it depends very much on the situation horse and rider are in at the time. The horse needs a steady contact to give it stability and security, but if it becomes unbalanced, it needs the freedom of its neck in order to regain control of its body. Should the horse lose impulsion and the desire to go forwards, the rider can release the contact to encourage the horse to get going again.

Contact does not mean bringing the horse's head down, so much as asking it to flex at the poll. The biggest fault the rider makes cross country is to shorten the reins if the horse get behind the bit and drops the contact, thereby shortening the neck and making it harder for the horse to balance.

Half-halts cross country

Half-halts are crucial to the training of the horse. There is not one exercise in the instructor's repertoire that does not require half-halts. They make the horse attentive to the rider and prepare it for the next situation that arises. They improve impulsion, contact and co-ordination of the aids, and bring the horse under control.

When riding half-halts, all the aids are used, but not necessarily all at the same moment. It takes the feel of the rider to use split-second timing of how much to use and when. In transitions from trot to walk, the timing of the aids is different from that from canter to trot, and different again when taking off before a fence or landing afterwards. They are different before a corner from before riding a volte.

Event rider Christopher Bartels is a master at applying half-halts in a light seat when riding cross country. The weight aids are used instinctively as an immediate response in every new situation. He is able to give half-halts in different ways, such as putting more weight in the stirrups, straightening up his upper body, or leaning back or forwards when going up and downhill, while still remaining relaxed and in control, and able to give the reins away as required. Sitting in the saddle prepares the horse for something new. The horse will learn over time that if the rider sits, it needs to pay attention and rise to the occasion. With experience, the aids can be given more quickly and more softly, developing a real partnership between horse and rider so that they are working together as a team.

This turn is inaccurate and the horse is falling on its inside shoulder.

This is a much better turn, with both horse and rider looking where they are going, and the bend in the horse's body can clearly be seen.

Riding turns

Riding turns accurately, in the same way you would in a dressage arena, is essential preparation for finding the ideal line of approach to an obstacle, both on a cross-country course and in a show-jumping round. The horse is straight when the hind feet follow in the tracks of the front feet, which is achieved by correct bending and flexion. The rider must keep his shoulders parallel to the horse's shoulders, and his hips parallel to the horse's hips. When turning, the rider's outside shoulder is brought slightly forwards, and the outside hip slightly back, keeping the outside leg position behind the girth to support the horse.

Turning correctly requires precision. It is achieved by using accurate weight aids, in a similar way to how a cyclist would turn on a bicycle. It is important to look in the direction of travel.

When turning, the outside rein should support the outside of the horse in conjunction with the outside leg. The outside aids should not be applied too strongly. The horse must still be allowed to bend and stretch through the length of its body around the rider's inside leg.

These basic rules still apply when riding up and downhill. When riding cross country, it is not a great problem if the horse is flexed slightly to the outside, as long as its body is bending around the rider's inside leg. It is more important that the inside rein remains soft and is not used strongly to turn the horse. The rider must continually check that the inside rein is light, so that the inside hind foot is not blocked from stepping forwards under the horse's body. If this happens, the horse will fall out through its outside shoulder. Giving the inside rein is one of the first things that any rider should be taught by his trainer.

When riding cross country or when show jumping, it is useful if the whip is carried in the outside hand. It can then be used as required as an alternative to pulling on the inside rein. The whip can get in the way a lot if is held in the inside hand, as it is the inside hand that needs to move in order to give the inside rein as required. Changing the whip into the outside should be practised, as it is important to be able to do this quietly and quickly. The inexperienced rider tends to concentrate so much on turning that he loses rhythm and the energy to canter on afterwards. A good exercise to use to make sure this does not happen is changing tempo within the gait on curved lines (see page 90).

Tips for riding turns:

- *Look in the direction of travel*
- *Outside shoulder forwards, outside leg back*
- *Give with the inside hand*
- *Be precise and ride accurately*

Stretching forwards and downwards

The exercise 'allowing the horse to stretch forwards and downwards' is just as important as being able to ride a half-halt. This is often done incorrectly, and frequently left out altogether when training older, more experienced horses. It is a key exercise to be used when taking a break during a training session, and to loosen up and cool off the horse before and after work. It is especially important for the event rider to do this. Riding forwards energetically, allowing the horse to stretch forwards and down, is the best way to correct many faults, such as losing rhythm and impulsion. Stretching builds trust and develops harmony between horse and rider.

These diagrams show stretching forwards and down, both incorrectly and correctly. In the picture above, the horse's head is behind the vertical and the nose is much too low. The horse's weight will be on its forehand and the gymnastic effect of the exercise will be lost. The lower picture shows the exercise done correctly. The horse's outline develops the neck and back muscles in the right way, and this is maintained by driving correctly with the leg aids.

Stretching forwards and downwards in a correct outline should be used frequently during training.

*The benefits of stretching
forwards and downwards:*

- *To consolidate the rider's skill*

- *To ensure the horse's training
  has been carried out correctly*

- *To test balance, suppleness,
  contact and rhythm*

Particularly when riding cross country, the rider should be able to give the reins in all gaits. Only in this way will horse and rider learn to stay in balance without relying on the reins for support.

*Common faults with stretching
forwards and downwards:*

- *The horse does not stay in front
  of the rider's aids*

- *The horse does not stretch correctly*

- *The hindquarters trail behind,
  putting the horse on its forehand*

- *Loss of contact and flexion at the poll*

- *Too small an angle at the jaw*

- *The horse jerks at the reins*

- *The horse comes behind the bit*

*These faults can be corrected
by riding correctly on turns and circles.*

This exercise teaches the horse not to rely on the rein contact for support in any gait. It is important to maintain the tempo and to keep the horse 'on the aids'. The rider should always be able to flex the horse at the poll and ask it to soften the jaw. This is achieved by stretching forwards and downwards, encouraging the horse to chew quietly on the bit as it does so. It is the only exercise where the horse's ears are not the highest point.

The outline is correct when the nose is forwards and down, with the horse's mouth level with the stirrup. The horse's head should be in front of the vertical.

Taking up the contact after stretching is an exercise in itself. The horse should willingly allow itself to be placed on the aids and worked in a rounded outline. Riding the horse on the bit and stretching again is gymnastic work for the back muscles, and develops strength and suppleness.

A misused exercise is stroking the horse's neck, where the reins are loosened momentarily to test the horse's self-carriage. Riders often move the hands forwards, but keep then too high above the horse's crest, so the contact is not released and the horse is held up by the reins. The rider must be able to release the reins at any moment, whether the horse is collected, bending and so on.

Training the horse

There are many books about training the horse in general. However, the subjects covered in this chapter are specific to cross-country riding.

Natural instincts and behaviour

The horse is essentially a plains dweller coming from the steppe and savannah areas, and is a flight animal by nature. It has survived for five million years and has not genetically changed to this day, though its use has evolved with man to its current status as a sports horse.

The natural habitat of the horse is out in the open, with good all-round visibility and little protection. Over time, fluctuations in the weather, poor climate conditions and great changes in temperature brought about a lack of food and water, causing the horse to change its choice of habitat. The horse is a herd animal and is seldom found wandering alone in the wild. Being sought as prey, the horse needs the protection of the herd.

To avoid beasts of prey, and to stay alive, the horse has developed acute senses, and efficient breathing and digestive systems to enable it to run at speed.

Spending the last 5.000 years in domesticity has not changed the horse's natural instincts, alertness and needs. This time span is only a short while in the horse's evolution. The psychology of the horse is very different from that of the human being. For man and horse to work together as a team, the rider must be able to put his own natural instincts to one side and think like a horse.

For the horse to make progress in its training, its surroundings and care are just as important as its schooling. The horse may develop problems simply because it is not cared for properly. Allowing a rider on its back is in itself a great feat of trust for the horse, whose natural instinct is to run away from predators. It is also important to take into account that in its natural environment, the horse spends most of the day wandering around grazing with the herd.

Things to consider when caring for the horse

- Keeping the horse in a stable where it cannot see out and has no physical contact is equivalent to putting a man into solitary confinement. However, stabling the horse in an environment where it can see and touch other horses is a necessity in equestrian sport, as it facilitates training. It is important, though, that the horse spends time out of its box every day. It is often not practical to turn a top-class horse out in a group in a field or barn if it is competing regularly, but it would be wise to do so during a break in training and at the end of the show season.

- The basic requirements of the horse are access to food and shelter from bad weather. Keeping it in a poorly ventilated stable does the horse no favours. It needs plenty of forage such as good quality hay and straw. It is best to feed the horse little and often throughout the day.

- In the wild, the horse's feet wear naturally as they move around. Problems in the horse's training are often caused by poor shoeing. Riders often omit to consider farriery as a possible solution to certain schooling issues. The best way of keeping the hooves in good condition is to leave them unshod. Regular trimming by the farrier is essential to keep them in shape. Working unshod cross country is perfectly feasible, even if the ground is hard or uneven. A young horse should be worked barefoot for as long as possible, as it becomes more surefooted. A horse without shoes is less likely to injure itself. Should the horse strike a leg, it will do less damage barefoot than when wearing shoes. Working barefoot strengthens the horn and improves the quality of the feet, making them easier to shoe in the future, should it be necessary.

- Living in the open has given the horse a great tolerance to extremes of temperature. The best protection for the horse is its own coat. Over-rugging the horse is often unnecessary and can be dangerous. However, it is important to cool off the horse gradually after exercise using a light, anti-sweat rug, especially if it is travelling soon afterwards. Wearing a light rug in the lorry, even in summer, can protect the horse from draughts and keep its muscles warm. The use of rugs depends on the breed of horse, the thickness of the coat and how sweaty the horse is. A rug made from natural material or a 'Thermo' rug are best at wicking away moisture from the skin.

"The ignorance of the rider is profit for the vet."
(Dr Karl Blobel)

The horse has to learn how to balance with a rider on its back, which is very different from its natural balance.

Anatomy and function

Working in the correct posture and outline is just as important for the rider as it is for the horse. It is the only way to work efficiently and easily, when riding either as a sport or as a hobby. The riding horse is taken more and more away from its natural instincts. For it to carry a rider's weight when moving around takes great trust in the rider and also physical strength. The horse's back was not designed to carry weight, so it is very important that the rider is able to remain in balance with the horse at all times. This is as important for the horse psychologically, as well as physically.

The riding instructor is responsible for the training regime that he sets for horse and rider. He is

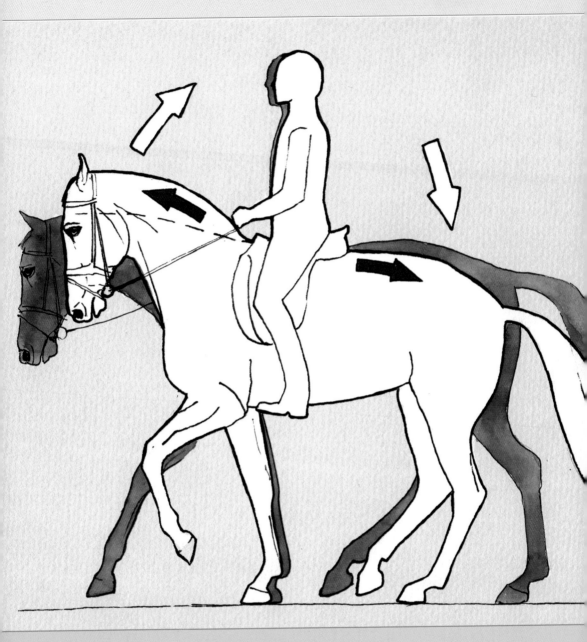

The reason for working the horse in a correct outline is to carry the rider easily.
The novice horse (the dark one in the background) is working in balance under the rider just as well as the collected horse. The difference between them is the collected horse's ability to take more weight on the hindquarters, lightening the forehand. The top line muscles that are used to raise the forehand and to lower the haunches are shown by the red arrows.

responsible for teaching them to move in balance, maintaining power and a correct outline. Establishing and maintaining a good outline requires knowledge of how the horse balances itself in nature, with an extended neck. Working the horse in an incorrect outline with a short neck and the nose behind the vertical has a detrimental effect both physically and mentally, as well as being extremely dangerous for both horse and rider. The horse will become afraid and this issue of working the horse 'over-bent' has a large question mark over it as poor practice and possibly as an issue of animal cruelty. It is just as much a responsibility for the riding instructor as the rider to discuss the effects of 'over-bending', which is a current news topic.

Riding well across country is all about balance. Correct balance enables the horse to work efficiently and powerfully. Impulsion creates better movement. Further strength is required to carry the rider in all situations. A good riding instructor will help horse and rider develop the skills required as an event rider by using appropriate exercises. It is important to develop the carrying power of the hindquarters and to ensure the correctness of outline. The rider must also be taught to ride in a good position in order to get the best out of the horse (see page 31).

In the early stages of the horse's training, covering basic education and familiarisation with new situations, one of the most important lessons is to learn to take the rider's weight on its back, which goes against all the horse's natural instincts.

The long back muscle has several functions. Not only must it take the rider's weight, but it also connects the hindquarters of the horse to the forehand, and is used to co-ordinate the horse's movement. As the horse's general muscle tone improves, then the job of the back muscle becomes easier. The nuchal ligament also plays an important part in the strength of the horse's back.

The horse is said to be strong in its back when it can work happily in a novice outline in all three gaits, i.e., with a gently rounded back with its nose just in front of the vertical. It should reach forward to the rein contact and be balanced enough not to lean on the reins. Cross-country schooling should be introduced as early as possible, with the help of a lead horse. This can give the young horse, and the rider, the confidence to go though water, over ditches, and up- and downhill.

"The young horse needs between six months and two years quiet gymnastic work. Only then is it physically mature enough to be called a riding horse."

(Dr Gerd Heuschmann)

In the early stages, the young horse will be able to get from A to B, but not necessarily in an ideal way. To go well under saddle cross country, the horse needs to develop the carrying power of its haunches, which it does naturally to a certain extent; but it needs to learn how to do this carrying the rider. For the horse to have the confidence to step under behind and to remain in balance, with the centre of gravity of horse and rider being the same point, the rider must maintain a steady contact at all times. Carrying power can be developed by riding alternatively uphill and downhill, as well as working on curved lines. It is important that correct flexion and bending are maintained during these exercises. It also helps to practise lengthening and shortening the canter stride. With careful training, the horse progresses and learns how to use its back properly. During this phase, the experienced rider will allow the horse to go at its own pace in a steady tempo, and support the horse with the aids. An inexperienced, and unbalanced, horse that has not yet learnt to halt is capable of going uphill. Going downhill is another story. The horse must be able to halt, and it should begin downhill work in walk, so it learns to take weight behind in order to remain in balance. Transitions between walk and halt will help the horse to remain on its haunches.

"The flexion of the haunches occurs when the joints of the hind legs bend, closing the angles of the joints during the support phase of a stride when the leg on the ground takes the horse's weight. The horse then pushes off with more impulsion, energy and elevation. This action of taking weight behind is described as collection."

(Dr Gerd Heuschmann)

Riding downhill and riding transitions between walk and halt teach the horse to maintain balance with its hind legs underneath it - this can be seen clearly here, even with an inexperienced pony.

Bending and lowering the haunches develops the pushing power required for both dressage and jumping.

The test of true collection is the correct rounding of the horse's back and its ability to stretch forwards and downwards (see page 42). At the first signs of difficulty, such as tightness through the back or an inconsistent contact, the horse must be taken back a stage in its training to re-establish the basics.

Signs that the horse's training is progressing in the right way are that the horse becomes more obedient to the rider's aids, and it becomes more supple and able to work through the back correctly. This is the culmination of following the scales of training. 'Throughness' develops from the combination of impulsion and suppleness. There is no short-cut to training a horse. A horse must be straight and able to work from behind, through its back and into an even contact. A crooked horse cannot work in this way.

Calm-forwards-straight

There are several references in this book to straightness and bending. The natural crookedness of the horse (as well as the rider) must be corrected by riding the horse straight. Gymnastic bending exercises are the way to straighten the horse and to improve suppleness. A crooked horse loses all pushing power from behind and will waste a lot of energy. Riding the horse truly straight and bending it properly result in effortless forwards movement and quiet riding.

"Ride your horse forwards and straight."
(Gustav Steinbrecht)

The horse is straight when it is bent uniformly from its ears to its tail. The hind feet should step in the prints of the front feet. Straightness and bending are two subjects that are closely linked together.

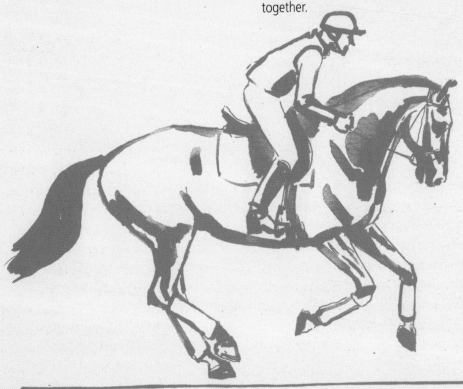

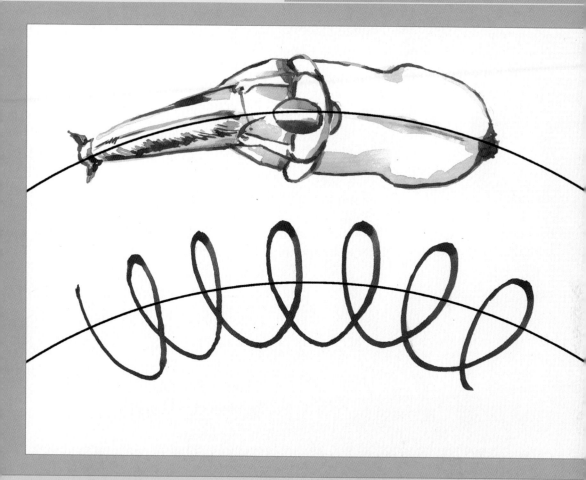

A supple horse can place its hind feet in the tracks of its front feet on straight and curved lines.

The riding instructor can explain the difference between longitudinal bending and the bending of the joints of the hind legs, or lowering of the haunches. Work on longitudinal bending with a horse being retrained begins on the lunge. On the lunge the joints of the inside hind leg have to bend, developing engagement. The horse has to bend through its body as it is worked on the circle. Lunge work prepares the horse for cross-country riding by increasing suppleness, improving straightness and developing the pushing power from behind.

In around 1750, Guérnière developed the movement 'shoulder-in' to improve the straightness and bending of the horse. This is an important exercise for the eventer.

"The art of riding has one goal, which is to make the horse supple, obedient and submissive and to set it on its haunches, whether it is a military, hunting or school horse and make its movement more comfortable for the rider to sit to."

(Francois Robichon de la Guérnière)

Cross-country equipment for horse and rider

In all equestrian sport, it is important to use the right equipment. This is fundamental for the event rider, where safety is of high priority. Protection for the rider is as important as for the horse and it must be ensured that the tack fits the horse properly.

Equipment for the horse

Saddle

The rider's contact with the horse it through the bridle and saddle. The saddle must fit the rider as well as the horse's back and it must not move when the horse is in motion. The saddle must be the right length for the horse's back in order for the back muscles to function properly. It is futile to buy a saddle off the peg, and very important that it is fitted by a qualified saddle fitter.

A dressage saddle is unsuitable for jumping, cross-country riding or riding an inexperienced horse, as it does allow the rider to establish a secure jumping or forward seat. A good general-purpose saddle can be used for training the young horse and for hacking out, but it best to purchase a proper jumping saddle for serious cross-country riding.

The saddle fits the rider when he can sit on the flattest part of the seat when riding with short stirrups. The knees must be in the correct place behind the knee rolls to ensure a secure lower leg position. Extra knee rolls situated above the knee and behind the calf give extra security for the rider's leg position. The deepest part of the seat should not be in the middle, but further back. If the rider tries to sit in the middle of the saddle, he risks developing a 'chair' seat. Trying to ride like this can cause muscle tension and limit the move-

It is important to have a saddle that fits both horse and rider.
The rider must feel safe and comfortable in order to ride the horse well in all situations.

ment of the rider's lumbar-sacral joint. This makes it impossible to follow the movement of the horse's back. This has a knock-on effect for the horse, which will also have limited movement in its back, and will lack suppleness.

It is important that the stirrup irons are wide enough and heavy. There are various types of safety iron available, but the most important priority is that the rider's feet do not become stuck in the stirrups. There are various types of saddle cloths to go under the saddle that wick away sweat, regulate the temperature of the back and prevent the skin and coat being rubbed. The saddle cloth will also muffle the use of a short whip behind the leg. The saddle girth should be a traditional one with buckles. It is important that it is in good condition and lies comfortably behind the elbows so as not to rub the skin.

Bridle

There are many different types of bit available from tack shops. A simple jointed snaffle is ideal in most cases. A thick bit lies still in the mouth and is comfortable for the horse. Bits are made from many different materials, which is a matter of personal choice and trial and error. A double jointed bit with a lozenge in the middle, sometimes known as a training bit, lies over the horse's tongue and is comfortable for the horse. A straight bar bit is not suitable for cross-country riding unless it is made from soft material.

A Fulmer snaffle with cheeks can prevent the bit sliding through the mouth, but it works just as well to use a simple snaffle with rubber bit guards.

"It is not the bit that cures everything,
but correct riding."

(Klaus Balkenhol)

If the noseband is not fitted correctly, and does not encourage a mild contact with the bit, then the muscle underneath the neck can become over-developed. This can happen particularly with a drop noseband. It is a very useful noseband for the young horse, but it must be fitted so it lies on the nose bone, above the nostrils so it does not interfere with breathing. As the horse progresses in its cross-country training, it would be advisable to change to a cavesson noseband so the horse can breathe more freely. It is important that the horse has time to get used to a new noseband.

The reins must be comfortable for the rider to hold and of good quality. Many riders feel safer with thick, heavy reins, but thinner, lighter ones encourage the rider to maintain a light, feeling contact with the horse's mouth.

A Fulmer snaffle is useful for cross-country riding as the cheeks prevent the bit sliding through the horse's mouth. (Photo: Christiane Slawik)

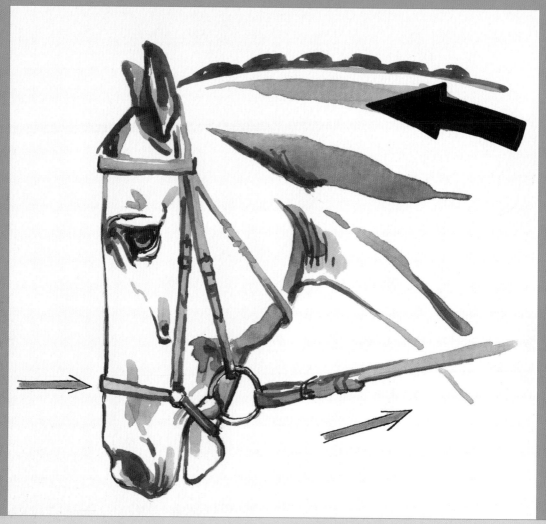

A correctly fitted drop noseband encourages the horse to take a mild contact with the bit. The pressure in the chin groove prevents it from opening its mouth too wide and resisting the contact. A horse that resists tightens its upper neck muscle and loses flexibility at the poll.

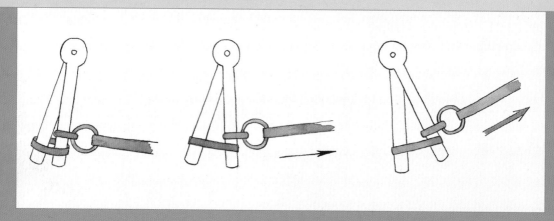

Studs

From a safety issue, it is advisable to fit the horse's shoes with studs. The horse will be much more sure-footed during competitions, or when introduced to new training exercises. This helps both horse and rider to be confident in their work. Studs are just as useful on hard ground as soft, and for coping with uneven surfaces and slippery slopes. During training, however, the horse needs to learn to balance, so it can cope with varied ground conditions without studs.

Artificial aids and equipment

One of the most useful artificial aids is the running martingale. No other auxiliary reins have a place either in the school or on the cross-country course. Alternative training methods are seen too often and have no place in correct training. The only time auxiliary reins should be used is as an aid to teach the horse to work more through its back, and even then they should only be a temporary correction and not over-used.

> "There is no artificial aid that will save the rider work."
> (Sheila Wilcox)

A martingale should only be used in certain situations. Here you can see how the martingale can prevent the horse from stretching its neck when tackling a drop fence. (Photo: Gero Kärst)

A correctly fitting breastplate ensures that the saddle stays securely in place, and gives the inexperienced rider a hand-hold over the withers.

Even a correctly fitted martingale can prevent the horse from stretching properly over a drop fence, so it is important to know when it should be used and when not. A martingale can prevent the horse from throwing its head up, but this should only be used as a correction by an experienced rider.

A martingale can be used for safety reasons when hunting or hacking out, but not out of habit. The rider must know what he is doing. A breast plate is useful to prevent the saddle slipping back. Often,

this has a martingale attachment, but this can be removed. The neck strap of a martingale or a breast-plate can be used to hold on to when riding in a light or forward seat, and this can be helpful for the less experienced rider. It should be fitted correctly so there is no danger of the horse putting its foot through the strap under the chest, and snug enough for the rider to have a secure hand-hold. The breast plate can be made of leather or elastic straps.

There are many types of leg protection for the horse on the market. Bandages are used for veterinary reasons, and should not be required by a fit and healthy horse. Brushing boots can protect the horse from minor injuries, but they should be used with care and fitted properly. The proper boots for cross-country riding do not come off even when sodden with water. Over-reach boots can protect the horse from stepping on itself, but again they must be fitted properly.

Equipment for the rider

The most important item of equipment for the rider is a correctly fitting helmet that complies with the current safety regulations. Check with the rule book of your national equestrian body for details. It must be so comfortable that you can forget you are even wearing it.

A back protector is another essential piece of equipment, and again, this should comply with safety regulations and be comfortable to wear. It is important that it fits the rider in the same way as the saddle should fit the horse. The body protector should protect the vital organs, but should not hinder the rider when going over obstacles. Problem areas with some body protectors are the arm holes and the coccyx. Modern materials wick

Every horse and rider is different, but it is important that the equipment used fits the individual properly

away sweat and also keep the body warm. Never buy a body protector without trying it on first.

Whether you use full-length leather boots or jodhpur boots with chaps is a matter of personal preference. Long-distance riders often travel sections of the course on foot, so it is important to have footwear that is as comfortable to walk in as to ride in. In competitions, leather or rubber boots are often allowed, but leather chaps are also permitted in some cases. Do check the rule book, though. Spurs do not often fit well when using short boots with chaps, so this should be borne in mind. The whip and spurs are artificial aids that are commonplace in competitive sport. They are also useful for schooling purposes and for hacking out. A whip more than 75cm in length should only be used for corrective measures. It should have a knob so it is easy to hold and does not slip through the hand. A hand loop is not necessary, as this makes it difficult to change the whip into the other hand quickly when changing direction (see page 41).

The shank of the spur should be a maximum of 3.5cm in length and must have a blunt end. Other types of spur are not necessary, either for training or competition. The voice is the most useful aid of all and is often more effective than any spur or whip (see page 39).

A good pair of gloves is an essential part of the rider's clothing, and they should fit comfortably. They should be made of material that wicks away sweat, and afford a good grip on the reins, should the reins become wet and slippery. They should be easy to clean.

Warming up and cooling down for horse and rider

In every type of competitive sport, it is very important to warm up and cool down at the beginning and end of every riding lesson, for the sake of maintaining health and fitness for both horse and rider. Every training session should start slowly and build up as it progresses. Cooling down allows the horse's breathing and heart rate to return to normal and the muscles to relax after work.

Warming up and cooling down should also be included when riding cross country, as well as short breaks during work.

The effects of warming up

The aim of warming up is to warm up and loosen the horse's muscles in preparation for work. Working quietly also relaxes the horse and prepares it mentally. This is the best way to protect the horse from injury or stress.

During warming up, the blood flow is increased to the tendons, joints, ligaments and muscles, and the joints are lubricated by joint fluid. This process takes about 20 minutes. Warming up improves the horse's suppleness, movement and strength.

A well-planned warm-up phase is essential for the horse's health and well-being.

The effects of warming up:

- *Raising body temperature*
- *Improving efficiency of the internal organs*
- *Improving efficiency of the nervous system*
- *Improving co-ordination of the nerves, muscles and tendons*
- *Increasing blood pressure, encouraging sweating and sensitising both horse and rider (for the rider this means acquiring a feel for the horse and its reactions to the aids)*
- *Establishing a correct outline so the muscles are functioning properly*
- *Encouraging excretion of waste products through the kidneys, liver and spleen*
- *Increasing respiration rate and depth of breathing*
- *Oxygenating the blood, which prevents tiredness and increases energy levels*
- *Improving strength and the desire to go forwards*

When riding out, there are many natural mounting blocks available. It is even better if you have a helper to hold the stirrup on the other side to prevent the saddle from slipping.

Loosening up work

Warming up is an assessment of the horse's wellbeing.
Other aspects of daily management that are important are:

- *How the horse behaves in its stable – whether it is settled or restless*
- *How it eats and drinks – does it eat its food?*
- *Droppings – how many and consistency*
- *Inspection of the limbs, back and hooves*
- *Regulation of pulse, respiration and temperature at rest (see page 126)*

67

Loosening up during the warm-up phase is in three stages: preparation, outline and strengthening (see overview on pages 72 and 73).

Preparation, loosening up and increasing awareness between horse and rider can be achieved by grooming, walking in hand or working from the ground or by lungeing. The horse should be encouraged to chew the bit quietly and to stretch down and relax during this work. Free-schooling and free-jumping are not classed as warming - up exercises, as they do not loosen the horse up, but require preparation in their own right.

To correct one-sidedness in the horse, it is necessary to work it regularly on the 'wrong' or right-hand side; most horses are handled from the left-hand side. Mounting from the off-side is a good exercise for both horse and rider. It is best to use a mounting block of some description to do this.

To warm up the horse's back and accustom it to the saddle, it is a good idea to spend 10 minutes walking on a long rein. This also gives the horse the chance to have a look around and relax.

'Warming up is often misunderstood. It is not about setting off for a chat and having no regard for the horse. Warming up is not common knowledge. Unfortunately, many riders are taken by surprise when they learn that warming up has nothing to do with a simple trot.' (Helmut Beck-Broichsitter)

In cross-country riding, all the muscle groups are used in the same way as in any human sport. It is important to take time with the first stage of warming up in walk. It is up to the rider to feel when the horse is relaxed and ready to commence work in trot. The next stage is to ride in rising trot, and then to sit for a few steps at a time to regulate the rhythm, and to ensure the horse is going calmly, forwards and straight. This requires the horse to work into a light, steady contact. The horse should be in a low, rounded outline, and stretch forwards to the rider's hand.

Early canter work should be carried out in a light seat on long reins to help the back muscles to loosen up. Most horses find it easiest to relax the back in canter. In trot and canter it is easy to keep the horse forwards. The tendons, joints and muscles loosen up during gentle exercise, which prepares then for the work phase. Riding quietly up gentle hills is very good for warming up and for increasing the body temperature, as well as helping the horse to establish correct posture and outline.

Introducing fitness work during the warm-up phase requires planning. After each fitness exercise, the horse should be allowed to relax and stretch. Cross-country riding in an outline uphill should be followed by riding on a long rein downhill. It is important that the horse be allowed to stretch forwards and downwards, chewing quietly at the bit (see page 42).

Fitness work will increase the horse's respiration rate, so it important to allow the horse's breathing to return to normal again afterwards.

Further development of fitness and stretching work should be done according to the scales of training, using carefully thought-out gymnastic exercises. The rider must know the horse in order to plan a suitable daily training regime to include gymnastic work, jumping exercises and grid work. It takes experience to plan a well-thought-out programme. It is better to vary the work with short sessions of each exercise than to work for too long on one thing. Forward-thinking thoroughbreds that are responsive and alert concentrate better if warmed up in a steady canter. During basic training, hacking out and work on tracks is very beneficial to this type of horse (see page 126).

Warming up is different for every horse. There is no fixed regime, and it is up to the individual as to what suits the horse best. In any case, warming up should take about 30 minutes, but it does not necessarily have to start with a long time in walk. With a young horse, the training session should end when it has achieved looseness and is able to work through the back. Horses that do not work every day require a longer loosening - up session. Warming up for a competition is different from for a training session, as it also depends upon the regulation of the heartbeat and respiration rate. This is where the inexperienced rider needs to enlist the help of his instructor.

Rest and relaxation

Working periods of rest and relaxation into the training programme is very important, especially with interval training. A recovery phase adds variety to the work, and can be helpful to relieve tension or a lack of willingness (see page 27).

There are many different ways of taking a rest during training. Walking on a long rein can restore rhythm and suppleness in all gaits. It is useful to take a break between different exercises, and also after a successful session. This also rewards the horse for a job well done.

Allowing the horse to dawdle along on a loose rein has no part in training, and is not what a rest phase should be used for. Relaxation work should improve motivation and create a willingness to start a new exercise.

Walking leisurely on a loose rein is not always the best way of having a rest during training. Rest phases should be carefully planned.

Cooling down and aftercare

Cooling down after exercise is equally as important as warming up, and allows the muscles to relax and to stretch. This process helps to prevent injury. It gives the body organs of the body a chance to rest and enables them to work more efficiently when put under pressure in the next phase of training. Sufficient time should be allowed to relieve physical stress and to allow the breathing rate to return to normal.

The first part of cooling down can be done either in canter or trot on a long rein, and this should be followed by work in walk on a long rein. The horse should not be washed down with cold water to reduce body temperature, as this can be a shock to the system. The muscles need time to relax, and the body organs must be allowed to excrete waste products, such as removing lactic acid from the muscles. The body can only be efficient if both the warm-up and cool-down phases are taken seriously and carefully planned. The cooling down phase can end with a spell in a solarium, so that the horse cools off slowly. Being turned out in a field to roll, graze and unwind is just as beneficial for the horse and very good psychologically. If the horse has time to relax properly after training, it will be fresh and keen to work the next day.

The length of the cool-down should be roughly the same as the warming - up phase. It can take up to 30 minutes for the horse's pulse and respiration rates to return to normal. It is very important to cool down properly after a competition. The horse needs time to recover physically and mentally from the pressure of competition. It is not good for the horse to dismount in a hurry and start preparing to leave. The fitter the horse is, the more quickly it recovers, and it should be offered hay or other roughage, which will help it to relax further. Hard food should not be given until later on, and then only in small portions.

Aftercare for the horse:

- *Keep the muscles warm and allow the horse to cool slowly – do not wash down with cold water*

- *Start cooling the horse's legs first, namely, the joints and tendons*

- *Wash off dirt and sweat with warm water*

- *Walk off until dry – a horse-walker is useful*

- *After about an hour (rugged up), water and hard feed can be given*

- *Check for strains and injuries*

Warming up and loosening up cross-country can help to mobilize the whole body.
All the muscle groups are used, in the same way that fitness training prepares a sportsman for his particular field of sport.
It is a very effective way of warming up the horse in a relatively short space of time without the horse becoming too tired.
It can be a very good idea to introduce the horse to water during this time when it is relaxed.. (Photo: Gero Kärst)

Schedule for warming up, cooling down and aftercare

Phase	Time measurement/Theme	Content
1	Twenty minutes **Preparation:**	• Groom, tack up, do up the girth loosely • Leading in hand or work from the ground in walk and trot • Tighten the girth • Lungeing and/or walking on a horse-walker • Free-schooling or free-jumping a warmed-up hor • Tighten the girth a second time, mounting with a mounting block and allowing the horse to stand still (thinking time) • Tighten the girth again
2	Ten minutes **Mobilisation and stretching:**	• Work in walk (allowing the horse to stretch) • Work on a long rein, putting the horse on the aids, loosening exercises • Straightening work, aligning the hindquarters and forehand
3	About fifteen minutes **Stretching and strengthening work:**	• Riding in all gaits, including canter work • Loosening exercises • Repeat frequently work on a long rein • Roads and tracks, cross-country obstacles (hill work, water, slopes) • Cavaletti and ground poles, gymnastic jumping
4	About five minutes **Check equipment:**	• Check the saddle girth, adjust stirrup length • Gather your thoughts – is everything going to plan?

Phase	Time measurement/Theme	Content
5	**About thirty minutes** **Stretching and strengthening work:** (Page 77)	• Work according to your weekly training plan • Interval training, rest phase • Loosening and supplying exercises for the young horse
6	**About twenty minutes** **Cooling down and aftercare:**	• Alternate cooling down with relaxation (taking the pressure off) • Canter quietly (one minute), steady trot (five minutes), walk (five minutes), then walk in hand • Care of the horse (washing down with warm water, replacing body salts with electrolytes, feeding firstly with roughage – hay – and later feeding hard feed in small amounts, checking for injury)

Variations to this routine can depend upon:

• Type and breed of horse
• Stable management conditions
• Skill of the rider
• Weather conditions/time of the year/daily timetable
• What the rider has planned to work on
• Variety in the work (to maintain willingness)
• Place (training area or competition venue))

Cross-country work

Riding cross country either as a sport or for pleasure has many applications in the world of equestrianism, as mentioned in the first chapter.

It has a place in eventing, hacking out, long-distance riding, hunting and so on. It should be a part of every horse's basic training.

Aspects of basic training that can be worked on when riding out are:

- *Working in a light or forward seat*

- *Riding over varied terrain, up and downhill in all gaits*

- *Canter work – developing a feel for the correct tempo, changes of direction, etc*

- *Introducing cross-country obstacles*

- *Building fitness and condition*

Comprehensive guidelines for cross-country training

To train horse and rider to ride cross country, a suitable training area is necessary. The requirements of the cross-country course are as important as those for a dressage or show-jumping arena. It should include a good ground surface, well-constructed obstacles and varying terrain such as hills and slopes that allow horse and rider to train safely for uphill and downhill work. If you are lucky enough to have good hacking that you can use, then natural debris such as fallen trees makes suitable obstacles, and you should encounter a variety of ground conditions. Every puddle or hillock is useful.

You will not often be able to work on flat ground. This has the advantage of getting the horse fit and familiarising it with different situations, making it surefooted and confident cross country, and teaching it to work efficiently and in balance. These criteria are all to do with developing trust and confidence in the rider, which are essential to successful cross-country riding.

You do not always need a cross-country course to get the horse used to different situations and to add variety into the training, but you do need a flat area or field for canter work.

The following training plan for cross-country work is basic schooling for any discipline of equestrian sport. It helps to also have a schooling plan for the arena or school, and to make a weekly training schedule to follow (see page 77). Days are numbered to be consecutive, so that the rider can plan his own schedule.

This plan varies the type and place of work and may be in the indoor school, outdoor arena, jumping arena, race track and so on, and may require the presence of a trainer. The training schedule may be altered due to inclement weather, or because the horse needs a change. The time of year can also affect it.

Weekly training programme

Day 1	Jumping	Grid work, riding parts of a course, also cross country fences, up to 30 minutes of jumping work
Day 2	Cross country	Canter/gallop work (see also training programme, pages 127 and 128). The aim is to establish a correct tempo and rhythm, and surefootedness over uneven ground.
Day 3	Dressage	Increasing the time spent out in the countryside, riding with short stirrups, a few exercises, up to 30 minutes of proper dressage work.
Day 4	Free day	Repeat any work that needs to be done again, practise working at competition speed, free jumping, practise water obstacles, in-hand work or ground work, having specialised instruction, go to a competition.
Day 5	Cross country	Basic training, roads and tracks, riding up- and downhill, water obstacles, uneven ground, steps.
Day 6	Dressage	As Day 3.
Day 7	Rest day	Leisure time, social contact, ride out, walk in hand, carriage driving. Turn out with other horses, grazing in - hand, (but not on rich pasture). Do not use a horse walker.

General tips:
Daily turn-out, particularly with other horses, is good for the horse. To build condition and fitness, a second daily activity session is required, comprised of activities such as those mentioned for the rest day.

Unfortunately, too much importance is placed on riding in competitions. The brief thrill of competing is not as satisfying as the enduring satisfaction that comes with producing a well-trained horse. (Photo: Johann Wachruschew)

The canter is a quiet, calm gallop that is balm for the soul and the horse's back

The seven days of the week can be switched around as necessary. This can change from week to week – you do not need to jump every Monday. It may be necessary to alter the programme so that the two dressage days follow each other. There is a quote from Xenophon that says,

"A weekly gallop where the horse gallops freely so that it sweats is of great benefit." *(See fast work, page 85.)*

Here is an explanation of the building blocks of the weekly training programme.

Hacking out or going for a ride out every day is useful when you need to vary the training programme. It is a good way to warm up, loosen up or cool down. It can also be useful on the free day or the day off. The advantage is that the competition horse gets out and about, encounters different things, and learns to concentrate better on the rider. This is also important for the other disciplines of dressage and show jumping. As with any other work, the aims of hacking out are to develop the horse's ability to work through its back, submission, and establishing purity of gait. For these reasons, it is a form of gymnastic work. Rods and tracks are part of the sport of eventing and this type of work builds condition and fitness as part of basic fitness training. (See summary, page 126.)

Canter work means to work at a quiet, calm pace, so the horse is on the aids and works without too much pressure. The canter is the equivalent of jogging for the athlete. You should be able to jog without becoming out of breath. Canter work in a steady rhythm once or twice a week is as important for the horse's health as is the daily turn-out. It helps to keep horse and rider, thinking forwards in their work. Cantering in a light seat is balm for the soul and for the horse's back. It is important that the rider is secure in the light or forward seat and can keep control of the rhythm and speed. The tempo and duration of the canter work should be worked into the weekly training programme. (For further information on canter work, see page 85.)

- Work in the indoor or outdoor school usually entails dressage or show-jumping training, which are the most common forms of training for most horses by their riders. Many of the aims of training can be achieved in the school, especially using exercises that develop suppleness, 'throughness' and submission. However, it would be beneficial for both the horse and rider to spend at least some time outdoors, warming up and cooling down in the fresh air. A short hack of about 30 minutes, twice a week, would add variety and a change of scene to the horse's regime.

- Working in-hand, lungeing and free-jumping are all educational for the horse and good for character building. A horse can be taught a new exercise before it is introduced under saddle, and all aspects of training can be reinforced to ensure the horse understands what is required. In-hand work develops the understanding of contact between the rider's hand and the horse's mouth, but work in-hand is not an easy option; it is just as much work for the rider as riding. It takes experience and knowledge to carry out in-hand work, lungeing and free-jumping proficiently and to avoid making mistakes. Lungeing is proper work for the horse and is not about running the horse around on the end of a long rope.

- A free day can be used to repeat any work that needs to be done again, to practise working at competition speed, flying changes and water obstacles, to have specialised instruction, to go to a competition and so on.

- A rest day should be worked into the training programme for the benefit of both horse and rider. It gives the rider a chance to have some free time and a social life, and gives the horse a break and a chance to relax.

- Entering a competition is often the main reason for training the horse. There is often too much importance placed on winning rosettes and 'pot hunting'. Focusing just on competitions and not on the aims of correct training is not what good riding is all about.

Cross-country work in all gaits

You need experience to ride cross country. This is not only for safety reasons, but also to retain the horse's trust at all times. Making mistakes will affect the horse's confidence and progress.

Riding cross country over uneven ground in all gaits begins in the walk, so that the horse encounters every puddle or small log quietly and calmly. Exercises can be introduced while hacking out, such as riding small circles around trees, cantering on flat ground, riding through an old gravel pit, going through water and so on. It may be helpful to have the assistance of a trainer with this.

Different exercises to improve the balance of horse and rider should be introduced, such as riding at a different tempo and changes of direction, especially in the light seat.

Hill work

In the next stage of training, hill work should be introduced on a regular basis. Riding up- and downhill should precede riding over uneven ground. This type of work is quite specialised, and there is no gymnastic jumping work or training in the school that can replicate it.

A sloping schooling area can be either round or oval in shape and offers endless training possibilities. Riding on curved lines on a gentle up- or downhill slope is excellent gymnastic work. It is very good for alleviating stiffness and tension, but it is important to make frequent changes of rein.

Uphill and downhill – the concertina effect

The benefits of uphill work are an improved outline, thrust, and the strengthening and stretching of the muscles, while downhill work improves collection and the bending of the haunches.

Alternating between uphill and downhill work has a concertina effect on the horse, as it is constantly changing its centre of gravity. Horses that are not used to this type of work tend to jog uphill and to hollow their backs when going downhill. Regular work in the sloping school can help to alleviate tension, backing off and other such evasions, and to improve suppleness, 'throughness' and submission. It also helps to develop the horse's trust in the rider and its self-confidence. Balance and skill are also improved. The rider learns to go with the movement of the horse and to ride more effectively. The horse can work more easily if the rider can maintain a quiet and balanced seat at all times. A good seat ensures correct flexion and bending, and accurately ridden gymnastic exercises, with the horse stepping under behind properly. The weight aids help the horse to engage its haunches when going downhill, both in trot and canter. It is important to keep the hands quiet at all times. This can be all practised in the sloping school before going out on the cross-country course.

Controlling the horse's impulsion up and down over hills is no mean feat, and involves changes in the horse's balance and centre of gravity. Many horses start to go uphill too fast and then run out of energy once they get to the top. The rider has to control the horse's impulsion to make sure it

Learning to ride downhill can be practised by riding on a sloping training area.
The rider learns how to sit in balance with the horse in relative safety..

does not ascend with too much speed, keeping the pulse and respiration rates controlled. Once over the top of the hill, the rider must ride actively forwards downhill, but not too fast, so the horse's breathing returns to normal quickly.

Riding up- and downhill using the length of the sloping school is quite strenuous for the horse. The training session should last no longer than 10 to 15 minutes, and it is important to change the rein frequently. The difficulty can be increased by going up a gait. Harmony can be restored in a quieter gait. The session should start with riding uphill first.

To build up the training
when riding up- and downhill:

- *Walk up- and downhill –*
  halt transitions when riding uphill

- *Trot uphill, walk downhill –*
  halt transitions on the way down

- *Canter uphill, walk or trot downhill*

- *Canter up- and downhill*

Uneven surfaces

Riding up- and downhill is preparation work for riding over uneven ground, banks or humps. Uneven ground demands quick changes from uphill to downhill. It is important to keep a rhythm when riding in such situations, as well as going up and down steps, through water, ditches and so on. This type of work improves balance and adaptability. The horse also becomes surefooted and safe to ride in all situations, and less likely to injure itself.

There are endless training possibilities to improve balance using ground poles, logs, ditches, steps, water obstacles and so on. Progress will be improved if a short break is taken between exercises by riding in rising trot, for example.

Fast work

Maintaining straightness and control in the canter or at the gallop is a test of training for horse and rider. This is exclusive to cross-country riding and cannot be rehearsed in the school. Canter work in the dressage arena or on the show-jumping course is different work. Here are two quotes that explain this:

> *"When rider and horse first learn to canter, it is considered a useful gait, and it is comfortable on long stretches, even more so than the trot. This is why I can do without trotting. If I have time, then I ride in walk; if I am in a hurry, then I gallop."*
>
> *(Count Lehndorff)*

> *""Pa-da-dam" is the sound of the canter – life is too short to ride walk or trot."*
>
> *(Hans-Heinrich Isenbart)*

Getting the canter right is the most important part of cross-country riding. First one has to learn to go forwards on the flat, and then to jump. Being able to canter for short spells and to jump single fences does not make an eventer or a show jumper. It takes more than one brick to build a house, and also requires the skill of an architect. Horse and rider need the help of a trainer to help them to tackle a cross-country course as a whole.

The purity of the gaits, including a correct canter, are as important to the event rider as they are to the dressage rider. An energetic gallop is good to freshen the gait and increase impulsion, and is enjoyable whatever discipline the horse is used for. Every horse should be able to work on a rhythm and be able to change tempo, and this depends upon using gymnastic exercises to improve the quality of the gaits. Enjoyment is the key to achievement, and this applies to any sport. The horse breathes in the rhythm of the canter. A good canter technique helps the horse to breathe efficiently.

"Riding dressage in a sluggish tempo without ever cantering or galloping freely forwards is detrimental to the function of the lungs."
(Martin Plewa)

If the horse is not ridden forwards enough in the canter or gallop, the contact can be lost and the horse does not work forwards into the bridle. If the horse does not work correctly into the bridle, then flexion is also lost. If the canter is on the forehand, this is usually a result of too strong a contact without the support of the leg and weight aids. Regular canter work alone will not correct these issues. The horse must receive further training.

With young or inexperienced horses, it is difficult to correct faults in the canter solely on the cross-country course. You may be able to control the speed and rhythm, but it is not unusual if the horse jumps around a bit and lacks concentration. The horse may become disunited and unbalanced or change the canter lead. This can be due to the rider being insecure in the saddle, uneven ground, puddles, other horses, going past the exit or a change in tempo. These issues need working on and can be tackled separately, where the horse is ridden past the exit in both directions, or ridden through puddles, and so on until it can do so without jumping around.

Concentration and condition

A great degree of concentration and fitness or condition is required for horse and rider to gallop cross country over a planned route at a designated tempo so the horse can breathe easily in the rhythm of the gait. This is mentioned many times in this book, and is an important part of the training programme (see pages 126 to 129).

One of the biggest causes of loss of condition is pain, which can be caused by the rider's mistakes or a faulty position, tack that does not fit properly and incorrect training.

Schooling in the sloping arena, and alternating between riding uphill and downhill improves the balance of horse and rider.

Learning to gallop

For horse and rider to learn how to gallop in balance, training should begin at a steady canter. It should be carried out on level ground working on a large circular route, such as a race track, so no changes of direction are required. The gallop is often ridden at too fast a pace to start with. This can cause the horse to go on to its forehand. A steady competition speed of 350 metres per minute is a good speed at which to maintain impulsion, rhythm and tempo.

"Most people believe that impulsion is when the wind whistles past your ears. Impulsion begins first of all with collection."

(Alois Podhajski)

Maintaining direction, balance and rhythm over uneven ground on a cross-country course requires training. Changes of canter lead when changing direction (flying changes) can be introduced when the horse changes leg of its own accord.

This is often easiest over a jump. Simple, inviting fences are very useful for this. The best way to tackle gallop training is to do it twice a week regularly throughout the whole year. Rhythm and control are far more important than developing speed initially.

Learning to gallop without a specific timetable

- *Developing scope, stamina, distance, and tempo by the feel of the rider and the experience of the trainer, to suit current training on an endless line.*

Suggestions on building up the work:

- *On level ground without changing direction*
- *On level ground with changes of direction*
- *On uneven ground over different surfaces and over humps in the ground with and without changes or rein*
- *Introducing two or three inviting fences with or without changes of rein*

Learning to gallop with a set timetable

- *Two minutes ridden twice on a set route, with a tempo according to feel.*

Suggestions on building up the work:

- *Gallop for four minutes two or three times*
- *With or without changes of direction or tempo*
- *On level or uneven ground or humps, with or without obstacles*
- *It is difficult to correct a flat canter or hand-gallop if the horse has no natural spring in its stride. It is best to start again with a better stride and a better seat. With interval training, two to three (two-minute) gallop sessions should be included.*

Developing the correct tempo

Once horse and rider can work at a steady canter, then they can start learning how to control the tempo of the canter. Tempo training is best done on a stretch of ground that can be timed with a stopwatch, and horse and rider can canter for a full minute. Initially, timing the canter is the job of the trainer. Once the rider can use his own stopwatch without upsetting the horse, then he can do it himself. The aim is for the rider to maintain a specific tempo with or without timing it. Every horse is different, and this must be taken into account when working out the optimum speed. Depending on the type of horse and its stage of training, it is best to start with a cross-country speed of between 350 to 400 metres per minute. The speed can be increased gradually to 600 metres per minute. Once the horse works comfortably and confidently at a slow speed, the tempo can be increased. Further increases in tempo can be made gradually. The higher the tempo, the more ground is covered by the horse. With interval training, the canter should be timed in one-minute intervals for two to three minutes in total. A good tempo to start with is 400 metres per minute over a canter stretch of between 800 and 1,200 metres in length. The success of the training session depends upon the co-operation of the horse. This exercise can include work over obstacles, on tracks and on curved lines.

Increase the difficulty of tempo training:

- *On even ground without changing direction*

- *On even ground with changes of rein*

- *On uneven ground and over humps with or without changes of direction*

- *Including two to three inviting fences*

- *Increasing the speed in increments of 50 metres per minute*

Changes of tempo

Being able to alter the tempo as required requires skill. It requires the ability to drive the horse forwards and to bring it back again easily, depending on the situation at the time and the type of obstacle facing the horse. The aim is for the horse to be able to respond by lengthening and shortening its stride to a slight change in the rider's weight. The rider should not need to use a lot of effort to achieve this.

Training begins with developing a shorter stride in a working canter. Shortening the canter should be done with the weight aids. Once this can be achieved, the horse will quickly learn how to go forwards in an increased tempo. The horse should come back with the weight aids to a shortened working canter. Increasing the tempo should just be done in short bursts. The horse should do this willingly, and be easy to bring back again. It should not just go faster; if this happens, it will run out of energy when going uphill.

Changes of tempo can be practised on a large circle or on curved lines. At a later stage it can be done on the straight. The hose should be ridden forwards and back again about every fifth stride.

This can be trained in the school by changing tempo every quarter circle or halfway up the long side.

In the beginning, the horse may lose balance. If this happens, the horse may become disunited, canter on the wrong lead or fall on its forehand, especially on straight lines. Frequent changes of rein and different exercises can help to correct this.

Transitions can be made in quick succession with between two and four ridden close together to make the horse more sensitive to the aids. This helps to bring the horse off its forehand and improves its balance. At a later stage this exercise can be done cross country with transitions at specific marker points.

Once the tempo can be changed easily without the horse relying on the reins, and the horse can come back and go forwards when asked and when ridden in a light seat, then it is ready for developing the feel of the tempo. This involves being able to maintain a specific tempo over a specified distances and at certain points on the cross-country course. At an earlier stage of training, this would be done over a set stretch of 20 to 50 metres. The tempo can be increased in increments of 50 to 100 metres per minute, but when on a cross-country course, this has to be done by feel, according to the ground conditions and the type of obstacle the horse is approaching. In order for this to be successful, the horse must co-operate with the rider and enjoy its work.

This horse, which is in the early stages of its cross country training, finds this relatively steep slope rather difficult: it is crooked behind and is trailing a hind leg, though it still manages to cope. In future, the rider should make sure the horse is straight on the approach which would make it easier for the horse. It is easy to see here how the muscles of the croup function.

Riding a cross-country course

When riding cross country, the same basic rules apply as when riding a show-jumping course. The exceptions are due to the different obstacles on a cross-country course and the nature of the course itself. These will be explained and clarified in this chapter.

Basic rules

A well-established canter and being able to ride on the correct line to a fence are the requirements of being successful on a cross-country course.

Different elements

A cross-country course is made up of different elements such as selecting the right line to a fence, coping with different obstacles, the ground conditions and natural situation of the course, the length of the course, selecting the right tempo to cover the required distance and tackling alternative fences. To cope with all this, the horse must have rideability and be well prepared through its training. Eventing, hunting, show jumping or taking part in any competition is not just a matter of combining these separate elements, but much more to do with building a partnership between horse and rider.

A good jump over a fence begins with the line of approach. It actually starts with the landing over the preceding fence; the landing after one obstacle is the preparation for the next. The approach to a jump begins much earlier than the three or four strides just before the take-off point. When planning the approach to a jump, three questions should be asked:

Where am I approaching?

Where and how will I take off?

Where will I go afterwards?

Here is a perfect picture of cross-country fences being tackled stylishly, economically, safely and comfortably.

Riding the correct line to a fence requires the same accuracy as riding dressage movements, and the figures on the ground are the same, but in a cross-country situation it is more difficult. There are no specific marker points at which to plan the next movement or exercise as there are in a dressage arena. Choosing the best line of approach cross country also depends upon maintaining rhythm, riding into the jump in an appropriate manner, safety and maintaining the horse's well-being. Every jump that is tackled wrongly destroys the horse's trust and disturbs the rhythm.

Balance, tempo, rhythm, and riding the correct line cross country and over fences all have their foundation in the scales of training. In the same way as riding a show-jumping course, the canter stride need to be shortened and lengthened as required over specific distances. On the cross-country course, the differences are often greater due to the difficulty of the obstacles and the length of the course.

The effect of the course on the canter stride

- *A distance becomes longer when the canter stride is shortened: for example, when going uphill, on heavy going, on slippery ground, on hard, unforgiving surfaces, through water or over narrow jumps. The key in these situations is to ride forwards.*

- *A distance becomes shorter when the canter stride is lengthened: for example, when riding on level ground, going downhill, on good going and when the ground is secure underfoot. The key in these situations is to reduce the tempo.*

Simply riding forwards is not always the solution to coping with awkward distances. There is the question of maintaining a steady tempo and collection, especially with water obstacles, difficult combination fences and drop fences. Impulsion must also be maintained. The way to cope with emergencies is to ride forwards in a controlled manner. The higher the tempo, the more appropriate and accurate the riding must be.

Technical jumping errors made by the rider are far more significant than the occasional mistake by the horse. It is the rider, not the horse, who has walked the course and studied each fence, line of approach, take-off and landing. A horse will learn from its own mistakes, as long as the rider is not a hindrance. There are many ways to tackle a cross-country course, but the main aims are to do it stylishly, economically, safely and comfortably.

Tackling cross-country jumps on even ground

A 'normal' cross-country fence is either an upright or a spread with its approach and landing on a straight line. The aim of jumping training in preparation for cross-country fences is that the rider can control the horse both before and after the fence in every situation. A powerful and controlled jump is only possible if the horse is well trained firstly in dressage and has developed true impulsion, straightness, collection and works through the back correctly. The horse should be trained in changing the tempo and selecting the right tempo (see pages 89 and 90).

A line of fences can be on a straight or curved line. An ideal line of approach goes from the middle of one obstacle to the middle of the next. The line of approach depends upon the skill of the rider and the ride-ability of the horse and its preparation beforehand.

Incorrect bending and flexion of the horse affects its ability to stay on the chosen line of approach. Any deviation affects the distance between the fences and can make a difference to the length and number of strides. A common mistake when approaching a fence on a curved line is to allow the horse to fall out through the shoulder. This happens if the outside aids are not effective enough (see page 41).

Maintaining a hand-gallop between the fences is one of the most important safety aspects. This ensures a controlled approach to the fences, maintaining impulsion and rhythm. When the horse has not yet learnt flying changes, then it should be

The horse's range of vision: the green area is where the horse sees the best. It can see indistinctly in the white area, and not at all in the red area. The horse must be allowed to raise its head on the approach to a fence so it can judge the obstacle better.

On the approach to a brush fence, the horse is not sure what he is faced with, so the rider is sitting deeply to keep the horse forwards into the bridle, but at the same time allowing the freedom of the neck (1). The rider then tightens her seat and lifts her knees and heels (2 and 3). She manages to keep the horse in front of her aids, still allowing freedom of the neck before the take-off (4). However, the horse manages to put a short stride in before taking off, coming in deep to the jump. The rider gives the reins, which is correct in this situation, allowing the horse freedom of the neck. The horse's ears and expression (4 and 5) show that it is not really confident with this particular obstacle and is a bit 'sticky' with both take-off and landing (5 and 6). However, they both recover well and ride away from the fence, with the horse regaining concentration on the rider.

easy to bring the horse back to the trot in order to change leg. The horse will find it easier to stay on the line of approach and jump straight if the rider can remain quietly in the saddle in a balanced seat.

In the early stages of training horse and rider for cross country, it is a good idea to go over planks, poles or tree trunks lying on the ground to practise a correct line of approach. This type of exercises can be useful as a warm-up and to train the rider's eye for assessing the distance to a fence. It is good for the confidence of both horse and rider to practise riding towards an obstacle and away again in a hand-gallop. Slightly higher obstacles can be used at a later stage for riding in, where it is a good idea if the horse is allowed to raise its head so that it can judge the height of the fence better.

The horse may back off a fence if the rider is too intent in keeping its head down on the approach. It is a common fault in training and riding not to allow the horse to raise its head for better visibility.

It is wrong to over-ride the horse into a fence with a strong, pushing seat, especially on the last stride before take-off. It affects the fluency and rhythm. A strong seat should only be used as a last resort in an emergency. It should not be part of normal riding.

The rider should, however, sit close to the saddle on the approach, but keeping the head and shoulders back until the horse takes off. He should remain passive with the upper body and use the weight aids and half-halts to keep the horse in balance in preparation for take-off.

It is important that the rider does not get out of balance and in front of the horse's movement. This results in mistakes with the front legs and an insecure landing. On no account must the horse be allowed to back off from the fence. Neither must the rider ask the horse to take off too far away. It is best to leave it up to the horse whether to put in a short stride before the fence or not. This depends very much on the quality of the canter on the approach.

When the rider is unsure of the point of take-off, he has to decide whether he is going to interfere or leave it up to the horse. The skilled rider will turn away, then make a new approach maintaining impulsion and rhythm, and ride forwards to the fence at the right moment. In a competi-

Here, it is clear to see the horse's bascule and suppleness of its back and neck over this trakehner ditch.

tion, you will lose time, but this is better than losing the horse's trust, and affecting its progress. You may also put the horse in danger by getting it wrong. It is important to keep the horse on the correct line, in balance, at a suitable tempo and in a good rhythm. Riding a line of related fences requires more skill and experience than riding over single ones.

Over-eagerness is often a sign of fear, as the flight reflex kicks in. When a horse comes in too fast, it is only natural to want to hit the brakes, so that you can steady the horse sufficiently to drive it forwards again to the fence and away afterwards. A good way to cure this problem is to jump from trot, maybe riding some voltes (small circles) or figures of eight before the approach to calm the horse. It is important when riding cross country for the horse to have a proper bascule and to have a good leg technique over the obstacles. These issues are often forgotten when going at speed over fences.

Cross country, a safe landing is the most important phase of the jump. It is dependent on a calm approach, the style in which the horse jumps and the rider's position. After landing, when both front and back legs are on the ground again, the horse should be put back on the aids and ridden forwards in a steady rhythm.

Quite often the canter can become flat and too fast after landing. This is a result of poor balance and could easily result in a fall. The beginning from inexperienced horse must be kept in balance when jumping. An experienced trainer will be able to help the rider to correct the tempo and outline. It is very bad to resort to pulling on the reins on landing to try to control the horse and to put it back on the aids. It is far better to ride forwards to regain balance.

If the horse cannot go forwards fluently after landing, then the landing is said to be 'dead'. The jump was not made on a good rhythm and forwards impulsion was lost. Coming in to a fence without impulsion puts the horse on its forehand on landing. This can be a sign of fatigue or inexperience. In training, the horse should be taken back a stage and worked over grids, using gymnastic exercises to improve its ability and to correct its style of jumping.

Training over single obstacles and related fences also means getting the horse used to different types of fence. Cross-country fences can be uprights, spreads, drop jumps and combinations. The higher fences tend to be uprights. There are various forms of spread fence, such as ditches, and zig-zag fences can also be jumped as spreads, as can barrels, tables and so on. Brush fences, hedges, mangers and tree trunks can also be spread fences.

Jumping different obstacles on level ground is the same as tackling show jumps. Many cross-country obstacles cannot be clearly defined, so their approach depends very much on the rider's experience and the type of horse.

Basic rules for tackling
different types of obstacle:

- *Upright fences are often under-estimated. There is a danger of knocking them, so the ground line is most important.*

- *Spreads must be tackled with respect, but are often over-estimated. They are often easier for the horse than an upright. They require impulsion.*

Cross country riding introduces both horse and rider to a variety of obstacles such as natural stone walls, jumping over and into water, ditches, and so on. (Photo: Gero Kärst)

Typical cross-country obstacles

There is an endless range of types of cross-country obstacle, offering a huge variety of training possibilities. The only limits are the situation of the course and the environment; the only requirements are a good course builder and an experienced trainer. For a successful course up to competition standard, the obstacles must be well constructed and positioned according to the lie of the land. The following obstacles described are typical fences, not specially designed.

Typical cross-country obstacles

- *Jumping up on to a bank*

- *Drop jumps where the bottom of the drop is visible or not visible*

- *Jumps situated on a slope*

- *Vertical jumps that can either be ridden from an uphill or downhill approach*

- *Steps*

- *Terrace jump*

- *Table that can be jumped on to and off*

- *Wall*

- *Hedge*

- *Brush fence*

- *Ditches – dry or water-filled, open, or with rails over (trakehner)*

- *Water with or without fences in the water*

- *Combinations and alternatives*

- *Technical aspects*

If the horse has learned to trust its rider, then it is less wary of deep water.

Water obstacles and ditches

Jumping into water is not natural for the horse to do. In the wild, the horse would consider water dangerous. In the herd, some of the horses would be on lookout duty while others would drink. For a horse to gallop through or jump into water on its own without the herd looking out for it would be considered suicide. The only to ride a horse through water is to gain its trust. Once the horse considers its rider to be its 'herd leader', then it is possible to ride the horse through water, as it believes that its rider will protect it from danger and it will come to no harm.

The horse can become afraid if the water is too deep, the bottom surface is uneven or if is ridden carelessly or badly. If it has no confidence in the rider, it will consider the water dangerous. Trust must be established during training so that the horse has enough faith in the rider to cope with unfamiliar situations during a competition.

The horse owner or rider find it hard to believe that a horse cannot canter over a metre-wide ditch, yet it can leap a distance of four metres, and can have a canter stride of up to two metres. It helps here to push the boundaries, and take the horse out of its comfort zone. It is all too easy to see a huntsman in every shadow, or a dangerous animal behind every tree. Going over a simple ditch gives the horse enough reason to mistrust the rider as it is, without the rider's imagination running wild!

It can be useful to ride behind a lead horse. A horse will often follow another over a ditch, where it refused with its rider. It can help to lead the horse in hand over the ditch first, to establish the rider's 'herd leader' status. It can also be the case that as the rider sits in the horse's blind spot, it becomes fearful in new situations. Shouting, yelling and riding roughly do not help, because such actions replicate a prey animal attacking the horse,

A lead horse can give security to the inexperienced horse when jumping a ditch for the first time. This helps to avoid getting into difficulty.

which heightens the horse's fear of the ditch. Reacting in this way can affect the horse's response in other situations around the cross-country course, and it will become distrustful and afraid. A lead horse can offer the security that the herd would. Forcing the horse should be avoided at all costs. The horse has to lose its fear of water, ditches and other frightening things through proper training.

The way to build trust in the young or inexperienced horse whose instinct is to run away is firstly to familiarise it with anything new in walk, and approach it calmly. Give the horse a chance to stand so it can look at it and smell it. Allowing it to eat grass around the edge of the ditch can help the horse to realise there is nothing to fear. Giving treats while standing near the ditch is also a good idea. You could stand with the horse on a long rein and allow it to graze, or to eat an apple or carrot. The next question is whether the horse is best jumping an open ditch, which is easy to see, or a ditch under a jump, which the horse will not see until the last moment. The answer to this is up to the horse and how it assesses the situation. If the horse has not yet worked out what it has to jump then it may hesitate or refuse. If it has been allowed to look quietly at the obstacle first and realises there is nothing to fear, then it will jump calmly.

Once the horse has successfully jumped two or three times in succession from walk and trot, then it can be ridden in canter. Rhythm, suppleness and contact should be re-established. Rhythm must be maintained over more difficult obstacles. Fences can be made easier by the addition of a ground line, for instance. Ground poles can be used either before or after a fence. It is important to have a short rest on a long rein once the horse had done well, but timing this depends on horse and rider. If they stop for too long, beginning again is sometimes harder.

Jumping up and downhill

Jumping on and off steps, tables and terrace fences requires good balance. Before every drop or downhill jump, weight is put on the forehand, and this requires trust, courage and skill. It can often happen that the horse makes a 'dead' landing, or becomes out of control or bucks. If this happens, the rider must spend more time making sure the horse is properly on the aids and that the canter is more controlled.

When jumping downhill, the rider should maintain a light, forward seat in order to remain over the horse's centre of gravity. He should look around to assess the situation, then look straight forwards, and certainly not down at the point of landing: the same as any other fence. The lower leg must remain either vertical or slightly forwards towards the horse's shoulder for security on landing. This helps the rider to remain secure in the saddle should the horse stumble.

"Think optimistically, sit pessimistically."
(Christopher Bartels)

It is not the intention in this chapter to go into details on sitting back in the saddle, which brings the rider out of balance and behind the horse's movement. This seat puts too much weight on the horse's back, disturbs the fluency and restricts the movement of the forehand. It can cause a 'dead' landing.

This extreme seat should not be used in normal circumstances. The rider just needs to sit as though on the approach to a normal jump. Sitting backing in the saddle when tackling a drop fence should only be used in exceptional circumstances. If the

The correct and incorrect seat over a drop fence. To keep the horse in balance,
and to give it the best chance of a successful jump without making a 'dead' landing (top picture),
it is important to maintain a light forward seat in order to stay over the centre of gravity (bottom picture).

A good example of a secure seat when jumping a drop fence. This keeps horse and rider in balance on landing, and the horse remains lightly on the aids.

rider uses this seat too strongly at a drop fence, he will put the horse at risk, break the rhythm and disturb the horse's balance.

It is helpful to place the hands on the neck either side of the crest of the mane, in front of the withers. Resting a hand on the neck helps the rider to maintain balance and to go with the horse's movement. At a drop jump, the horse's neck will lower. It can be useful to make a bridge with the reins (see page 36) so the rider has a handle to hold on to the aid balance and to keep the hands still. Simply holding the mane can bring the rider in front of the horse's movement and out of balance. In the forward seat it is important to keep the lower leg secure, with the knees and calves securely against the horse, and the heels down. The weight should be kept into the stirrups. The hands should follow the horse's neck movement so they do not block the movement of the forehand, and allow the horse to use its back properly. This avoids a 'dead' landing.

Another problem with riding drop fences sitting back in the saddle is that the rider is pitched forwards on landing. This increases the risk of the horse stumbling, as too much weight is placed on its forehand. Similarly, looking downwards when trying to pick the line of approach can cause problems. It can make the obstacle look frightening, and the drop can seem deeper than it really is. The same applies looking into ditches. The rider should look forwards, not downwards. Looking down can result in the horse making a 'cat' jump. The inexperienced horse will jump up in the air at first when faced with a drop fence, which will disturb the rhythm and forwards momentum will be lost. For this reason, it is wise to approach drop fences from a walk or a quiet trot to encourage the horse to jump downwards, and not upwards. The oppo-site situation to this is the horse that slides down a vertical drop with its front legs extended. This is a risk of injury to the limbs. To jump safely, the horse must not be hollow in its back. Experienced horses will keep their weight on their haunches as they descend over a drop fence.

Riding forwards after landing should pose no problem to horse and rider, as the ground will always go uphill afterwards, which is far easier. Impulsion must be maintained when jumping uphill and a brisk tempo should be maintained. If the horse takes off too early when jumping up steps, for example, then the jump will seem wider than it really is. If the horse does not jump big enough, then the front legs will land too short on the step. If it jumps too big, then there is a risk of hitting the hind legs. As when jumping single fences uphill, care should be taken with steps to judge the distance correctly.

Jumping into water is similar to jumping drop fences. Maintaining a steady tempo and impulsion is difficult in water, as the horse's instinct is to get out quickly. It may jump about in the water as the spray hits its nose. A powerful, steady canter through water should be practised first, without any fences to jump. This a good type of work for building condition.

Tackling the take-off on to a bank, preparing to turn to the next fence on landing (this can be seen on page 112): immediately before the jump (1), the rider has the horse in front of her aids and the horse's attention is on the next phase of the jump. The rider is allowing the freedom of the neck with her hands. When landing on the bank (2), the horse places his forehand well forwards and has enough room for his hind legs to land on the bank (3).

Here you can see the gymnastic effect on the haunches. The horse has landed securely, and the rider is looking forwards to the next phase of the fence. As the horse jumps off the bank (4), the rider could allow the horse a bit more freedom through the neck.

On landing after the fence (5), the horse has the freedom of his neck once more.
The rider takes her centre of gravity back and rides the horse forwards. Both horse and rider are in balance when riding the first canter stride away from the fence (6).

Important rules
for different obstacles

- Jumping uphill requires plenty of impulsion and a regular tempo.

- A drop fence/jumping downhill requires courage, trust and balance. On landing, the rider must take his centre of gravity backwards, follow the forwards movement of the horse and remain supple. As the horse lands on its fore-hand first, it must be able to bring its hind-quarters under its body as soon as possible under its centre of gravity. If the horse is going to stumble, it often happens a stride or two after landing if horse and rider are unbalanced; it does not actually happen on the point of landing.

- A jump without a visible point of landing will cause the horse to back off. It is important in this situation to keep riding forwards, and to make sure that the horse does not become short in the neck or tense in the contact.

- Jumps on a slope where one side is higher than the other require accurate riding and the rider should have an answer to the following questions: Where am I approaching? Where will I jump? Where do I go afterwards? Cantering on a uphill and downhill slopes should be practised in training to make sure horse and rider can stay in balance. Practising also reduces the risk of injury. It is important to practise on both reins to work both sides of the horse equally. This type of work requires a surefooted, confident horse. Jumps can be sited on the side of a hill or bank.

- Jumps on a slope to be jumped up or downhill are the same as drop jumps or jumping uphill.

Most horses like jumping hedges. They are to be treated as spread fences and ridden towards at an energetic tempo and a lot of impulsion.

A slower tempo should be used when jumping downhill. The horse should not take off too early when jumping downhill. Nor should it take off too close to the fence, as there is a risk of catching the hind legs on the jump, and becoming unbalanced and stumbling on landing.

- Steps, terrace jumps and tables are the same as jumping up or downhill. These fences often cause a loss of impulsion.

- Hedges and brush fences are treated as spreads. Horses like to jump these with a bit of speed, so it is important to maintain an energetic tempo and ride with enough impulsion. The horse should always be ridden forwards, without going too fast, if the distance is awkward.

- Walls should be ridden in the same way as hedges and brush fences. A horse can try to 'bank' them (push off the top) so it is important that the rider has a secure seat. This should not be encouraged or practised in training. An experienced horse will work out for itself if it needs to 'bank' a fence or not. It is not usual for the horse to stumble.

- Open ditches, either dry or filled with water, need as much impulsion as a spread fence to prevent the horse from hesitating. Neither horse nor rider should look down into the ditch. The horse should concentrate on how to tackle the jump over the ditch. The rider should look ahead and be thinking, 'Where do I go next?'

- Water with a jump out should be tackled the same way as a jump into water. Water acts as a brake to the horse and often causes a fall, so cantering through water requires as much training as the fences do. Water spray makes the obstacle more difficult for horse and rider, especially with fences to jump, where it affects visibility.

- Water with a jump in should be treated the same as a drop fence. The water acts as a brake to the horse, and confidence is required as the surface beneath the water cannot be seen. It is very important to ride forwards after the jump, especially in water.

- Jumps with take-off and landing in water are basically the same as a single fence, but the rider must maintain impulsion. Jumps in water should be approached in a collected canter.

- Combinations with alternative options are a matter for the rider. The rider should choose a route that is best for the horse and should take into account the horse's capabilities. With alternative fences, the easier jumps are on the longer route, and the difficult jumps on the short route. This type of obstacle should be practised in training. In a competition, alternatives are a matter of trust between horse and rider. Being able to cope with them is a matter of experience. Every type of obstacle can be included in a combination. Coffins, Pulvermann's grab and sunken road are all types of these. When riding combinations, the horse must be able to collect as well as lengthen on request. The tempo should be steady to allow the horse to assess the situation and to see what it is jumping. This especially applies to coffins where the horse may see the ditch at the last moment and be taken by surprise.

- In-out obstacles are very useful in training. They are best composed of two fences set close to each other, to be jumped without a canter stride in between. On safety grounds, they are only included in competitions for the more experienced horse and rider. The two elements should be contrasting so the horse does not try to jump them as an oxer.

- Technical aspects of the cross-country course apply to the way it is ridden. The aim is that the horse that completes the course within the time allowed is the winner. A well-trained horse will have an advantage. For example, the rider will be able to turn more sharply into fences, ride shorter lines of approach on curved lines, be able to place the horse accurately on take-off, and keep the horse straight when jumping fences without wings. It is not obligatory for fences to have wings, and this should be practised in training. For horse and rider to have a good technique, it is important that the training follows the scales of training to establish tempo, rhythm and straightness.

- Jumping from light into dark and from dark to light requires a confident approach. In these situations, the horse's visibility is affected, but research states that horses can see quite well in the dark. The rider should bear in mind whether or not the sun is shining and if light is coming through the trees. Dappled shadows can affect visibility. Jumping from dark to light is easier.

Every type of fence needs to be ridden differently and places different demands on horse and rider. The first requirement is to practise collection, and to progress from easy obstacles to more difficult ones. It is important to train over different fences, in different combinations, and to cover all eventualities. Horse and rider should work up to jumping a course of different obstacles without stopping or losing rhythm. Obstacles can be simplified by adding a ground line either before or afterwards, for example. Should rhythm be lost, the rider should learn how to recover more quickly as training progresses. If a problem arises, then it can be overcome by repeating the exercises another time in a different place.

Every situation is different. When coming across a new jump, for example, there is a saying, 'Let him see and let him go'; in other words, take it as it comes. Training the horse for cross-country riding is about developing confidence, balance and surefootedness. The rider learns to trust the horse and to ask the right questions, so he gets the right answers. Eventually horse and rider learn to cope with all types of fence and all situations.

In this coffin combination, the horse can clearly see the ditch in front of it as it jumps the first element.

Fault correction

As cross-country training progresses, so faults that occur when jumping should be corrected. Mistakes in a competition are usually refusals, disobedience and falls. Mistakes are often caused by a faulty rhythm or tempo, by riding the wrong line of approach, taking off at the wrong place, landing poorly and so on.

After a fall, it is important to rebuild trust and to restore the partnership between horse and rider, and make them brave again. Depending on how experienced horse and rider are, it may help to enlist the help of an experienced trainer to help them recover from a fall. It can help to train on other exercises, to take their minds off the incident (see page 27) and restore confidence.

Careful, systematic training reduces the likelihood of a fall. Mistakes should be corrected as they happen, so horse and rider are not put at risk. Anger and impatience are not the way to do this. Correction should not be a battle (see page 25). The horse should be carefully and quietly ridden to overcome its fears. Remember that the mistake cannot be undone.

After a refusal, the horse can want to rush off, and this is often made worse by the rider pulling at the reins and pushing with the seat in his efforts to regain control. It would be more correct to work the horse on a circle until it is calm and to put the horse back on the aids. Riding at the fence without planning a correct line of approach and without forethought is bound to fail.

It is important that both horse and rider calm down. An experienced trainer can help with this. The horse should be brought to a halt in front of the jump on the rider's aids and allowed to look. The inexperienced rider should be encouraged to breathe deeply and slowly to calm the nerves.

They should analyse why the horse refused. Was the rhythm correct? Were the line of approach and striding to the fence accurate? Was the rider determined enough? These things should be thought over quietly after the training session.

> *Possible corrective measures after a refusal:*
>
> - *Turns on the forehand/haunches, demi-voltes in walk towards the enclosed side of the jump or a fence*
> - *Transitions to and from specific gaits (trot or a steady canter)*
> - *Making a fresh approach on a better line*
> - *Riding energetically forwards after a successful jump*
> - *Encouraging and praising the horse with a low, calm voice, keeping a contact with the mouth while patting it on the neck*

For a long-term correction, the rider must remain calm and take sufficient time. Once the horse is secure again on the rider's aids, then a further attempt can be made. It depends on the situation whether the same exercise is repeated or a new one is tackled. Once an exercise is successful, there is no need to repeat it again. Finish on a good note.

"There is no point in sacrificing the horse's willingness to learn for the sake of a certain exercise. It is best to finish the daily training too soon rather than too late. There is always another day."

(Colonel Williams)

After three unsuccessful attempts, but preferably after the second, you should stop. Horse and rider will have a mental block. This is highly likely in a competition situation where horse and rider are in the same circumstances, and probably due to a lack of trust and confidence. It can be useful to overcome the problem at a different time and in a different place. Later on, though not on the same day, it can be helpful to tackle the problem fence following a lead horse.

After analysing a specific problem, it can be helpful to approach the fence quietly from trot, rather than canter.

Basic work, training, and improving fitness and condition

In their basic training, horse and rider will have learnt to go cross country effortlessly, smoothly, safely and comfortably and become used to riding in the horse's natural environment. They can consolidate and increase their understanding of cross-country riding through a sensible training programme, increase their fitness by following a fitness plan, and put the training into practical use through competitions.

Explanation of terms

Basic training is the learning phase of training for horse and rider. Each single part of the training programme has its own goal. Once all these separate parts of the basic training have been successfully completed, then the real training begins. There is no training without basic training.

The purpose of **training** is to build upon the basic training and further develop the skills and experience of horse and rider. It can be useful to go on intensive training courses for a change of scene, and to have new experiences. During their basic training, horse and rider should have developed suppleness, confidence and strength. Further training will develop these skills and also develop riding at speed, co-ordination, endurance, stamina and other attributes. These are all necessary to ride combination fences, for example. In training, it is important to be aware of physical and mental fatigue. Any omissions in the basic training will come to light. It is important to take into account the age of both horse and rider when planning a training programme.

Criteria for successful training:

- *Maintaining a correct outline and way of going*
- *Maintaining health and well-being and enjoyment*
- *Appropriate training for horse and rider to achieve their goal*
- *A correct balance between the amount of feed and the type of work*
- *Caring for the horse properly after exercise*

Fitness training is beneficial for every healthy horse. It is fun and creates a lust for life. Ability can be improved greatly with correct training

as character, temperament, behaviour, resistance to disease and suitability for the work. A horse that is not blessed with all these attributes can develop through correct training into a quality animal. Basic training is beneficial to every healthy horse, as it is enjoyable and creates a lust for life.

Performance comes as a result of willingness and ability. Talent and the will to win are as important as having a good constitution and character. They will be developed further through appropriate and correct training. Surefootedness, confidence, and a fluent canter and gallop are essential, but they are not inherited. They can be successfully improved and developed with training.

Improving condition through training

There is no magic potion or feed supplement that is as beneficial to the health and well-being of man or horse as keeping fit and in condition. Condition or fitness training improves the function of the body organs and enables the body to carry out tasks more economically, with less effort and energy.

Condition means the ability of the horse to carry out the required work both physically and mentally. It is a combination of health, well-being, suitable training and the horse's constitution.

Constitution is the connection between body and soul. It is made up of different aspects, such

Training:

- *Improves respiration and pulse at rest*
- *Improves circulation and builds muscle*
- *Strengthens tendons, joints, ligaments, cartilage and bone*
- *Improves digestion and appetite*
- *Improves excretion of waste products through the liver and kidneys*
- *Maintains health and well-being*
- *Improves resistance to disease and infection, and promotes recovery from injury*

A fit horse has energy reserves that can be called upon when in circumstances that it has not encountered during training. This gives it a greater tolerance against injury, pain and sickness. An untrained horse can only reach 70 per cent of its potential. A trained horse can reach 90 per cent; the remaining 10 per cent is required for stress and self-preservation. This is only able to be utilised through doping. Doping raises the pain threshold.

Two natural indications of over-exertion or fatigue are pain and reduced ability. Pain-relieving drugs can disguise symptoms, so should not be given.

Man takes note of his personal limitations, such as tiredness, to reduce the risk of injury or over-exertion. The horse's willingness to work for the rider sometimes overcomes its natural instinct, and it will carry on even when exhausted. This does, however, depend on the type of horse.

A tired horse will quickly become lame. Tired muscles cannot support the joints on landing over a jump, or when taking each trot or canter stride. Tired muscles are no longer flexible and this is a cause of tendon problems.

Each spell of exertion puts the organs under pressure. Incorrect training and a lack of fitness causes degeneration. Not all the organs and body tissue are affected in the same way during training. The horse's lower limbs have poor circulation, which is difficult to improve. Long periods of slow work are the most effective and should be included in basic training (see page 123). A fitness programme should take into account ground conditions, especially in winter, and should be adaptable for use all year round. A healthy horse should be got into condition before serious training starts.

Time allowed during training for improving the condition of different organs:

- *Circulation: one week*
- *Muscles: about three weeks*
- *Tendons and joints: more than nine weeks*
- *Nervous system and resting pulse: more than one year*

The effects of training

Assessing the training process is as important as taking a correct dose of medicine or taking blood pressure, for example. The best way of regulating training is the feel and instinct of the rider. The rider must feel what the correct tempo is for the horse. The horse should be able to breathe easily, work in a correct outline, become supple and work comfortably when put under pressure. The rider has to know the individual horse. its character and eating habits, and should assess these before and after each training session.

Assessing the effects of training:

- *Character: alertness, freshness, well-being*
- *Eyes and ears: signs of good health*
- *How the horse utilises its food, whether it is a 'good doer'*
- *Willingness to work*
- *Good muscle development without too much fat*
- *A shiny coat, especially on the neck and shoulders*
- *Sweats freely – it should be watery and unscented*

Temperature, respiration and pulse are indicators of good and poor circulation, and of general fitness. An unfit horse will have far less stamina than a fit horse. More demands can be made on a horse in good condition without having a detrimental effect on its well-being. Taking the temperature, pulse and respiration rates as a matter of course helps to regulate the horse's health and to detect any problems early on.

The aim of fitness training is to produce a fit horse that recovers quickly during a rest phase. Pulse and respiration rates should return to normal after ten minutes rest: an unfit horse will need longer. Long-distance riders are accustomed to taking these on a regular basis during long rides to make sure they are travelling at the optimum speed for their horse.

The pulse should be taken immediately after exercise, before it has slowed down. It can be taken manually either on the inside of the jaw or the underside of the tail. The heartbeat can be checked with a stethoscope.

There are electronic indicators available on the market that can be worn under the saddle or on the girth, where they should be positioned by the elbow joint.

To avoid taking too many measurements, the rider must get a feel for the horse's state of fitness. Wearing an armband that shows relevant data can be useful to help the rider assess the horse during training.

The rider should take notice of early signs of lameness during training, and act upon them immediately by giving the horse two or three days off.

The rider must be aware of how the horse should feel during each week of training. He must not forget to progress steadily and must remember how important it is to build condition gradually in order to avoid problems.

Rates for pulse, respiration,
and temperature at rest should be:

- *Pulse: 28–40 beats per minute*

- *Respiration: 10–12 breaths per minute*

- *There should be four pulse beats*
  to every breath

- *Temperature: 37–38 degrees C*

At work (light to medium):

- *Pulse: 60–100 beats per minute*

- *Respiration: 30–75 breaths per minute*

- *There should be two pulse beats*
  to every breath, or one to one

- *Temperature: 37.5–41 degrees C*

During training,
the following should be noted:

- *Incidents during training*

- *Day, week, weather*
  (temperature, air quality)

- *Changes to the training plan*

- *Temperature, pulse and respiration*

- *Appetite, attitude, shoeing,*
  general impression, vaccinations, etc

Improving fitness through conditioning work

Improving the horse's fitness and condition is essential to maintain the horse's health and well-being during the long process of basic training, whatever their field of work is. Every kilometre ridden outside in all gaits, in all weathers, over varied terrain is the foundation for later success in all aspects of equestrian sport, including breeding. Fitness training is an important part of all equestrian sport. Regular cross-country training can reduce feed costs and fees for the vet and farrier. When re-schooling horses, fitness training forms the most important part and can be extended to 18 months or longer. Horses used for distance riding, breeding or for leisure all benefit from having a good grounding in their education.

Horses in riding condition at the end of their basic training, need at least eight to twelve weeks conditioning work to improve their level of fitness. The first level of improving fitness is to increase training time by repetition or by introducing spells of invigorating work. It is most important in cross-country training to learn how to regulate the tempo. This is a fundamental part of cross-country training and it can be done by using a stopwatch that is easy to read. Timing the horse should be done at the walk to start with. In conditioning work, the working tempo is the basic speed of the gaits. This differs from horse to horse, and should be monitored and altered as necessary as training progresses. Basically, timing the gaits over a set distance can easily be done while warming up.

It is important to learn the working tempo of the horse's gaits, so it is easy to tell if the horse is going too fast during training.

The rider should develop a feel for the correct tempo in all gaits. It can help to use a stopwatch and to enlist the help of a trainer.

The two cross-country days on the weekly training plan (see page 77) should be used for improving the standard of training with the help of an experienced trainer.

When training on roads and tracks, the rest phases can be for more than 10 minutes, and should be fairly frequent. This type of work can be introduced gradually from the fifth day of training. Ground conditions are important: on hard ground, the tendons and ligaments are used more; deep ground works the joints.

In canter work, frequent breaks should be taken lasting from two to five minutes. These should be ridden at the walk, to ensure that the horse does not become too tired. Training should alternate between work and rest periods, increasing and decreasing the demands on the horse over a long period of time. The work should be varied to avoid over-training any particular aspect. To keep the horse fit and well, and to use low-risk training, hill work, riding through water or up steps should be introduced as the horse becomes fitter. These types of work require stamina and the horse should be capable of fast work before attempting them.

Building up fitness levels when working up hills, steps, etc, should be done firstly at the walk, then in trot, and finally at a quiet canter. Climbing up hills should be done at a gait suitable for the hor-

se, and this is down to the feel of the rider, as every horse is different.

The intensity of work depends on the feel of the rider and his experience. Cantering uphill requires a faster tempo than riding on the flat, but raises the fitness levels more quickly. As the horse becomes fitter, the rest intervals become shorter as the horse recovers more quickly. The harder the work, the longer the rest should be.

Cantering through water requires special training due to the water having a braking effect on the horse. The horse must be got fit for this type of work. Training through water is useful preparation for encountering all types of water complex in the future.

The aim of fitness training is to improve the condition and capabilities of the horse, rather than chasing rosettes and winning prizes. Fitness training will get both horse and rider in condition, which prepares them for future training in any discipline.

Horse and rider should both be in condition after fitness training. They should be fit enough to

Cantering through water is a good way to build fitness levels and is an important part of basic training.

cope with most eventualities that they will come across when preparing for a competition. What is not guaranteed is whether the designated training requirements have been carried out.

Training schedules give guidelines of the required work and ensure that the horse remains fit, even through the winter months.

A healthy horse should never start training if it is not fit. Interval training is where strenuous work is alternated with easier work. It is a very effective way of getting the horse fit. Examples are given in the following training schedules. Canter training can be built up as per the schedule shown in the next box.

Canter/gallop training schedule

Aim: Fitness training or repetition

Goal: 4,500 metres in 10 minutes at a tempo of 450 metres per minute, allowing 10–20 per cent as reserve energy for unfamiliar ground, jumping, and other work

Work: one to two times a week, 10 minutes in a tempo of 450 metres per minute, plus 10 per cent = 11 minutes (or +20 per cent = 12 minute)

Building up gradually: start with 60 per cent (six minutes), increasing every two weeks by one minute: make sure changes of rein are included

Basic Training Schedule Road and Track

Aim: First fitness training during or following introductory training, also for repetition
Objective: Three 10-minute rides at 220 metres/minute achieved within 12 weeks
Training: During weekly schedule (page 77) once or twice per week. Rest every 10 minutes.
Use the remaining time to warm up and cool down, and for fitness training while hacking out

Week	Distance	Total minutes	Total distance	Hours cross country
1	5	5	1100	1:30
2	5	5	1100	1:30
3	5 – 5	10 +	2200	1:45 +
4	5 – 5	10	2200	1:45
5	5 – 5 – 5	15 +	3300	2:00 +
6	5 – 5 – 5	15	3300	2:00
7	5 – 5	10 -	2200	2:00
8	5 – 10 – 5	20 +	4400	2:30 +
9	5 – 10 – 5	20	4400	2:30
10	5 – 10 – 10	25 +	5600	3:00 +
11	10 – 10	20 -	4400	3:00
12	10 – 10 – 10	30 +	6600	2:30

Total				
	Distance: 220 m/min	> 3 hrs	> 41 km	
	Canter: approx. 350 m/min	3 hrs	63 km (estimated)	
	Trot: approx. 200 m/min	5 hrs	60 km (estimated)	
	Walk: approx. 100 m/min	15 hrs	90 km (estimated)	
	Total	**26 hrs**	**254 km (estimated)**	

+   = increasing difficulty
-   = decreasing difficulty
>   = more than
<   = less than

Example for 8th week:
    30 minutes   Loosing/warming up, hacking out cross country
     5 minutes   Work on roads and tracks
   10 minutes   Fitness training cross-country
   10 minutes   Work on road and tracks
   10 minutes   Fitness training cross-country
     5 minutes   Work on road and tracks
   80 minutes   Balance to total time – use for generel cooling-down exercises cross-country
Total: 150 minutes = 2:30 hrs

Fitness Training Schedule Canter 1

Aim: First fitness training following introductory training
Objective: Two 3-minute rides at 400 metres/minute achieved within 12 weeks
Training: During weekly schedule (page 77) once or twice per week. To cool down, 2 to 5 minutes walk or slow trot. Use the remaining time to warm up and cool down, and for fitness training while hacking out

Week	Minutes of Canter	Total Canter	Metres Canter	Total time Hours cross country	
1	2	2	800	1:00	
2	2	2	800	1:00	
3	2 – 2	4 +	1600 +	1:30 +	
4	2 – 2	4	1600	1:30	
5	2 – 2 – 2	6 +	2400 +	2:00 +	
6	2 – 2 – 2	6	2400	2:00	
7	2 – 3	5 -	2000 -	2:30 +	
8	3 – 2	5	2000	3:00 +	
9	2 – 2 – 3	7 +	2800 +	1:30 -	
10	3 – 2 – 3	8 +	3200 +	2:00 +	
11	2 – 2 – 2	6 -	2400 -	2:00	
12	3 – 3	6	2400	2:00	

Total	Canter: 400 m/min	1 hrs	24 km
	Trot: approx. 200 m/min	10 hrs	120 km (estimated)
	Walk: approx. 100 m/min	11 hrs	66 km (estimated)
	Total	**22 hrs**	**210 km (estimated)**

+ = increasing difficulty
- = decreasing difficulty

Fitness Training Schedule Canter 2

Aim: Repetition, to prepare for building higher performance condition
Objective: three 5-minute rides at 400 metres/minute achieved within 12 weeks
Training: During weekly schedule (page 77) once or twice per week. To cool down, 2 to 5 minutes walk or slow trot. Use the remaining time to warm up and cool down, and for fitness training while hacking out

Week	Minutes Canter	Total Canter	Metres Canter	Total time Hours cross country
1	2 – 2	4	1600	1:30
2	2 – 2 – 2	6 -	2400 +	2:00 +
3	2 – 2 – 2 – 2	8 -	3200 +	2:30 +
4	3 – 3	6 -	2400 -	2:30
5	4 – 4	8 +	3200 +	3:00 +
6	5 – 5	10 +	4000 +	2:00 -
7	3 – 3 – 3	9 -	3600 -	2:30 +
8	3 – 3 – 3 – 3	12 +	4800 +	3:00 +
9	4 – 4 – 4	12	4800	2:30 -
10	5 – 5	10 -	4000 -	2:00 +
11	6 – 6	12 +	4800 +	2:30 +
12	5 – 5 – 5	15 +	6000 +	2:30

Total				
	Canter: 400 m/min	1:52 hrs	> 44 km	
	Trot: approx. 200 m/min	10 hrs	120 km (estimated)	
	Walk: approx. 100 m/min	16 hrs	96 km (estimated)	
	Total	< 28 hrs	260 km (estimated)	

+ = increasing difficulty
- = decreasing difficulty
> = more than
< = less than

Overview of Fitness Training Schedule

Based on weekly schedule (page 77), fitness training schedule roads and tracks 2 (page 126), fitness training schedule canter (page 128)

Week	Day Date	Cross-Country training Roads & Tracks (R) Canter (C)	Dressage (D) Jumping (J)	Training protocol: Free day Rest day
1	1	---	J/arena	---
	2	C: 2 x 2 mins	---	---
	3	---	D/CC course	---
	4	---	---	Free day
	5	R: 1 x 5 mins	---	---
	6	---	D/CC course	---
	7	---	---	Rest day
2	8	---	J/CC course	---
	9	C: 3 x 2 mins	---	---
	10	---	D/arena	---
	11	---	---	Free day
	12	R: 1 x 5 mins	---	---
	13	---	D/arena	---
	14	---	---	Rest day
3–7		---	---	---
8	50	---	J/new location	---
	51	C: 4 x 3 mins	---	---
	52	---	D/new location	---
	53	---	---	Free day
	54	R: 2 x 5 mins, 1 x 10 mins	---	---
	55	---	D/CC Course	---
	56	---	---	Rest day
9–12		---	---	---

Always make sure to include warming and loosening up, as well as cooling down.
Keep in mind that training requires professional knowledge. Include two stints of exercises per day.

The schedule can be changed any time or adjusted to objectives of training

Successful cross-country training is essential for enjoying a great day out with the hunt. (Photo: Beagle-Meute Lübeck)

Benefits and outlook

Fitness training benefits the horse's quality of life overall, whether horse and rider are preparing for participation in events or not. In any case, it gives a solid grounding for every type of riding activity.

It is useful for distance riding, for which stamina is needed. Hunting gives the opportunity to canter and gallop in a group behind a pack of hounds, for which cross-country training is invaluable. Horse and rider should be well prepared for riding with the hunt so they can enjoy the occasion.

Part of the fascination with this splendid form of equestrian sport is that the route the hunt takes is undetermined and horse and rider will be going across unfamiliar territory. For this reason, it is important that horse and rider attend training sessions, and learn how to cope with the unknown before galloping with the hunt.

The event rider does not take part in as many competitions as the dressage rider or the show jumper, due to the demands on the horse. A good level of fitness is essential up to intermediate level. Having a good experience at a competition is as important as sound basic training. It is essential to train over a proper cross-country course to get the necessary experience in between competitions with the help of an experienced trainer. The different phases of the competition should be practised, such as the roads and tracks. Galloping on a race track is useful. The rider should be familiar with the format of the competition. This should be covered in basic training.

Roads and tracks should be covered at a tempo of 220 metres per minute. This can be affected by the ground conditions and the rider should learn tactics to deal with this. This means working at an energetic trot, but does include some canter and walk, focusing on the importance of loosening and warming up. In the following are some suggestions illustrating the advantages of hacking out before a cross-country ride.

Advantages of riding on roads or tracks before a cross country ride:

- *Riding independently, without the trainer's or parents' help, on long tracks alone in the countryside prepares for the cross-country ride*
- *Avoid jumping and too many friendly encounters between horses in the warm-up arena*
- *Inexperienced competitors can start off more relaxed without having to wait*
- *Fewer horses queue up around the start*
- *Possibility to build first fences towards home, the warm-up arena or car park*
- *The rider can learn to be punctual*
- *Possibility to use the wider vicinity of the event, instead of clogging up the start, finish and warm-up arena, creating a more relaxing atmosphere*

It is the rider's responsibility to work the horse sensibly so it does not become exhausted and at risk of injury or an accident.

Final comments: doing the right thing, limits and goals

If horse and rider do not ride outside on a regular basis, it is natural for them to be anxious when riding cross country. These people do not give the horse a chance to become familiar with the outdoors. Even horses that are usually easy to ride and of a calm disposition can become fresh and want to buck and leap around if kept cooped up in the stable for too long. This can be difficult for the rider to sit to and cause a fall.

Regular daily work in the school or jumping arena is essential for the horse's well-being and to keep it safe to ride. Cross-country riding is only dangerous when the horse's care and training are not suitable or sufficient for the individual. This is what this book is about!

The riding horse is a modern creation by man, and it is important to consider the horse's natural instincts and requirements when caring for it. The horse owner should be self-critical and take the blame for mistakes. Horses should be carefully trained for sport so they do not end up in a zoo, or even worse be put down, because of their owners' ignorance.

The riding instructor is responsible for teaching the rider how to progress with the horse safely, comfortable and effortlessly. His aim should be to promote the longevity of the horse's career.

The rider should be competent. This means the acquisition of knowledge, feel and experience. A competent rider makes a good horse trainer, and will not often require the help of an outsider.

The aim of training is to improve the horse's rideability. A competent rider produces a confident horse that can work in self-carriage and enjoys life.

It is important to have regard for the welfare of the horse. The boundaries are often pushed to the limit in competitive sport through the demands and expectations of sponsorship deals. Many competition venues are so intent on putting on a good

show that they lose regard for the horse's natural behaviour. Competitions that test the rider's style and proficiency are important for maintaining a good standard of riding. It is the responsibility of the judge to assess whether horse and rider have been trained properly or whether they are just performing the test on the day. The same goes for training the cross-country horse; cutting corners and not spending enough time in proper training can only be detrimental to the sport.

Back to the aim of basic training: a horse with a correct way of going is easy for the rider to sit to, and it will be comfortable and safe. A horse working in a correct outline will work for the rider easily and not against him. The horse will go freely and willingly forwards.

Cross-country riding is useful in many ways. Horse and rider develop harmony, confidence and security. The light seat allows freedom of the horse's back and lets the horse move naturally forwards with 'the wind in its nostrils'. The horse becomes more rideable, surefooted, faster and fitter and more beautiful as a result.

"Ride your horse out in the sun and fresh air! Leave the dusty, narrow school with tight corners for narrow-minded people!"
(Rudolf Georg Binding)

A great sight: harmony between horse and rider, showing great trust and confidence cross country.

Appendices

List of quoted people

- **Bartels, Christopher** (born 1952), successful international dressage and event rider, trainer of the German Eventing team since 2001
- **Beck-Broichsitter, Burkhard** (born 1949), international cross-country course builder
- **Beck-Broichsitter, Helmut** (1914–2000), event rider and author
- **Binding, Rudolf G.** (1867–1938), author of traditional prose
- **Blobel, Dr Karl** (born 1935), former team vet to the German Eventing Team
- **Bürkner, Felix** (1883–1957), founder of the Olympic training quadrille 1936, trainer at the cavalry school, Hanover
- **Caprilli, Federico** (1868–1907), founder of the modern jumping seat and the light seat
- **Durand, Pierre** (born 1931), Director of the French Cavalry School at Saumur
- **Festerling, Günter** (born 1932), Riding Master, head of the German State Riding School in Warendorf, 1972–1976
- **Frederick II. The Great** (1712–1786), King of Prussia
- **Guérinière, François Robichon de la** (1688–1751), to this day, the figurehead of classical riding
- **Habel, Max** (1910–1989), member at the Cavalry School, Hanover, team trainer to the German Event Team 1968–1980
- **Heuschmann, Dr Gerd** (born 1959), vet and author
- **Holck, Count Carl Friedrich Erich** (1886–1916), one of the best riders in Germany since 1900, and the first rider to employ the new light seat, developed by Caprilli
- **Müseler, Wilhelm** (1887–1952), influential influence in equestrian sport
- **Niemack, Horst** (1909–1992), international training-judge and former chairman of the German judge-union
- **Plewa, Martin** (born 1950), Head of the Westphalian Riding and Driving School, National Eventing coach 1984–2000
- **Podhajski, Alois** (1898–1973), former Head of the Spanish Riding School in Vienna
- **Seunig, Waldemar** (1887–1976), rider, trainer, judge, equestrian author
- **Seydlitz, Friedrich Wilhelm von** (1721–1773), Riding General of Frederick the Great
- **Steinbrecht, Gustav** (1808–1885), Classical Riding Master of the 1900s
- **Trumler, Eberhard** (1923–1991), anthropologist, cynologist, dog trainer, author
- **Williams, Colonel**, British riding instructor (around 1960)
- **Xenophon** (430–354 CE), pupil of Socrates, politician, writer, philosopher and founder of hippology
- **Ziegner,** (briefly Albrecht of) (born 1918), international teacher of all disciplines
- **Ziethen, Hans Joachim of** (1699–1786), Riding General of Frederick the Great

References

Bartels, Christopher/Newsum, Gillian:
Training the Sport Horse
J. A. Allen, 2004

Binding, Rudolf G.:
Das Heiligtum der Pferde
Gräfe und Unzer, 1953

Binding, Rudolf G.:
Reitvorschrift für eine Geliebte
Hans Dulk Verlag, 1948

Caprilli, Federico:
The Caprilli Pages
J. A. Allen, 1967

Dietze, Susanne von:
Balance in Movement:
How to achieve the perfect seat
Trafalgar Square, 2nd edition, 2005

Guérnière, François Robichon de la:
School of Horsemanship
J. A. Allen, 1999

Habel, Max:
Vielseitigkeitsreiten
Limpert, 1982

Heuschmann, Dr. Gerd:
Tug of War: Classical versus
'Modern' Dressage
J. A. Allen, 2007

Meyners, Eckart:
Effective Training and Riding:
Exploring Balance and Motion
Goals Unlimited Press, 2004

Müseler, Wilhelm:
Riding Logic
Eyre Methuen, 1973

Opel, Heinz von:
Eventing Technique
J. A. Allen, 1991

Podhajski, Alois:
Die klassische Reitkunst
Nymphenburger Verlag, 1965

Steinbrecht, Gustav:
Das Gymnasium des Pferdes
Cadmos Verlag, 2001

Xenophon:
The Art of Horsemanship
J. A. Allen, 1999

Ziegner, Kurd Albrecht von:
Elements of Dressage
Cadmos Books, 2005

Index

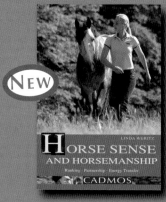